COMPANY REORGANIZATION FOR PERFORMANCE AND PROFIT IMPROVEMENT

Recent Titles from Quorum Books

Practical Strategic Planning: A Guide and Manual for Line Managers
William P. Anthony

Getting Absent Workers Back on the Job: An Analytical Approach
David A. Dilts, Clarence R. Deitsch, and Robert J. Paul

Practical Techniques of Business Forecasting: Fundamentals and
Applications for Marketing, Production, and Financial Managers
George Kress

United States Interest Rates and the Interest Rate Dilemma for the
Developing World
J. Pierre V. Benoit

Law and Economic Regulation in Transportation
Paul Stephen Dempsey and William E. Thoms

International Law of Take-Overs and Mergers: Asia, Australia, and Oceania
H. Leigh Ffrench

Office Space Planning and Management: A Manager's Guide to Techniques
and Standards
Donald B. Tweedy

Advertising Financial Products and Services: Proven Techniques and Prin-
ciples for Banks, Investment Firms, Insurance Companies, and Their
Agencies
Alec Benn

The Political Economy of International Technology Transfer
John R. McIntyre and Daniel S. Papp, editors

Fair and Effective Employment Testing: Administrative, Psychometric,
and Legal Issues for the Human Resources Professional
Wilfredo R. Manese

Office Records Systems and Space Management
Donald B. Tweedy

Managing Real Estate Taxes
Jerry T. Ferguson and Edward C. Spede

Strategies and Skills of Technical Presentations: A Guide for Professionals
in Business and Industry
James G. Gray, Jr.

The Management of Business-To-Business Advertising: A Working Guide
for Small- to Mid-size Companies
Stewart Halsey Ross

COMPANY REORGANIZATION FOR PERFORMANCE AND PROFIT IMPROVEMENT

A GUIDE FOR OPERATING EXECUTIVES AND THEIR STAFFS

Stanley B. Henrici

Q Quorum Books
NEW YORK · WESTPORT, CONNECTICUT · LONDON

Library of Congress Cataloging-in-Publication Data

Henrici, Stanley B.
    Company reorganization for performance and profit
improvement.

    Includes index.
    1. Organizational change.   2. Corporate reorgani-
zations.   I. Title.
HD58.8.H46   1986   658.4'063   86–613
ISBN 0–89930–159–2 (lib. bdg. : alk. paper)

Library of Congress Catalog Card Number: 86–613
ISBN: 0–89930–159–2

First published in 1986 by Quorum Books

Greenwood Press, Inc.
88 Post Road West, Westport, Connecticut 06881

Printed in the United States of America

∞

The paper used in this book complies with the
Permanent Paper Standard issued by the National
Information Standards Organization (Z39.48–1984).

10 9 8 7 6 5 4 3 2 1

Contents

Preface

This is essentially a "how-to" book. In it I describe one systematic method of overhauling an organization.

In doing so I stick to the sequential processes of rebuilding. Abstract theories of organization, instructive as they may be, remain in the background, for my theme is not architectural aesthetics. Rather I am talking about structural engineering, cement mixing, and brick-laying. If you want to reorganize, what is the first thing you do to-morrow morning?

My field is both limited and diverse. Limited in that the book out-lines only certain specific procedures, to which many companies must have found alternatives. Diverse in that it applies to many more organizations than companies alone. Though I use the word "com-pany" what I say is often equally applicable to other organizations, whether religious bodies, government bureaus, or health and edu-cational institutions.

Throughout I have tried to emphasize that reorganization must consider not only company welfare but also human interests. It must have what our founding fathers embarking on a large reorganization of their own called "a decent respect to the opinions of mankind." Reshuffling a company is not like rearranging the insentient furniture in your office. It deals with people, and people make the company. So I have stressed the need for sensitivity to the problems of human reaction.

Many of the approaches and procedures described in the following pages were developed by James A. Foltz in association with JoAnne McLaughlin, both of whom I am indebted to for help. Additionally I wish to acknowledge with thanks the many examples of good practice that have been supplied by executives in commerce and industry. Unfavorable examples, where not otherwise identified, are fictions derived from general observations and do not refer to any specific persons or company.

COMPANY REORGANIZATION FOR PERFORMANCE AND PROFIT IMPROVEMENT

1

Before Reorganization

Sometimes a company can strangle in its own departments. Sometimes a company can try to reorganize and in doing so botch the job. Sometimes a company can, in the process of reorganization, repeat the very errors that made reorganization necessary in the first place. Sometimes a company....But let us look at an example.

Buck Gray, the manager of the Deaf Smith, Texas plant of an imaginary manufacturer of plastic hardware, needs an additional lift truck for his receiving dock, and since it will cost more than $5,000 he must send an appropriation request to the central office in New York. There his modest appeal follows a winding course through the headquarters departments. First it is logged in by the appropriations clerk, who promptly remands it to Gray because it has been typed on an obsolete form. On its return it goes to the capital budget department (properly budgeted?), the financial analysis department (ROI satisfactory?), the controller (preliminary approval), the safety department (all safety devices provided for?), the energy coordination department (kind of fuel?), the engineering department (design specifications?), the environmental department (fumes, wastes?), the material handling department (capacity and mast height okay?), the surplus equipment clerk (no trucks available for transfer from other locations?), the supplies department (spare parts included in appropriation?). the law department (terms of contract of sale?), the industrial engineering department (truck really needed?), the architectural department (floor load okay?), the credit department (vendor financially sound?), the planning department (long-range plans still include this factory?), the labor relations department (effect of additional mechanizing?), and the general manager of manufacturing.

At each of these departments the appropriation request lingers on desk tops. People are out of town, they have other things to look at, they want to digest and check its contents. Also, each person in the approval corps has a question or two. (For example, why can't Deaf Smith use a ten-year-old truck that is on the surplus list at Possum Mound factory?) Some queries are handled by phone, others by letter, with copies to everybody up the line in order to get them on record. It being hunting season in Deaf Smith, the chief industrial engineer schedules a trip there to make a study of the receiving dock. The safety, environmental, and energy groups revive an old debate about gas vs. electric, bitterness erupts, and the human relations department has to get them all together at an all-day off-site meeting to "articulate where they are coming from" and resolve their interpersonal conflicts. The material handling department, noticing that this truck replaces a small manual transporter, accuses architectural of having failed to verify that the existing dockplates will sustain its weight. "Dockplates," replies architectural, "aren't our problem. Take them up with the engineering department." The traffic department wonders if incoming materials shouldn't come in on slip sheets rather than wood pallets.

The art department sends a registered letter to Deaf Smith reminding the manager that the truck must be painted in corporation colors.

All this goes on for some months, engendering much thoughtful, conscientious, and certainly what zero-base budgeting would call essential work by a number of employees. In time the appropriation receives all its approvals and makes its way to the purchasing department, which dispatches yet another letter to Buck Gray: having just concluded a fleet agreement to buy fork lifts from another manufacturer, they cannot order the make of truck he has specified. But they have to, Gray writes back. Only the one he has requested has local parts and service facilities available. The correspondence drags on in fits and starts. But Gray doesn't care. The truck he wants has been darting about his receiving dock for the last year. He got it on a month-to-month rental, with payments applicable against purchase. This he arranged with his friend the local supplier, who is also and importantly, a member of the local board of assessors. Gray didn't get his job by being passive or by failing to understand what goes on in the central office departments of his company.

In the meantime president George Brown, tall, whitehaired, florid, and imposing, is occupied with larger matters. He has been brought aboard to improve the company's unsatisfactory return on its investment. "One thing I've noticed here," he says in a meeting with his vice presidents: "This company's awash in paperwork. It's a paperwork parlor. We've got to take a hard-nosed stance, I mean bite the bullet and get down into the nitty-gritty." To this end he appoints a committee, or task force as he prefers to call it, charged with reducing the number of printed forms circulating among the offices. "Fewer forms, fewer people," he says. "This is the opening gun in a total reorganization." The task force enthusiastically conducts a series of meetings at a local conference center. In them it describes its overall mission, reduces this to objectives and then to specific goals, devises an overall strategy, outlines tactics and follow-up checks, draws up a PERT chart to guide its campaign, and embodies the lot in a thirty-two page report to Brown. This Brown reads with some satisfaction in the company plane on his way to a conference at Boca with his sales and marketing vice presidents. He approves it and the task force takes a first step: gathering information as a basis for action. It distributes to all employees a form on which they are to record all the forms they use and the time spent in (1) reading, (2) entering information, and (3) abstracting information. It also issues another form on which employees are to make suggestions for form reduction. And to meet long-range needs it sets up a new department, "Forms Management," with a manager and two employees "to restrain future forms proliferation." A wave of hilarity sweeps through the company. Buck Gray, in a fit of whimsy, sends in a deadpan suggestion for a form to authorize any new forms. The task force, greeting it with appreciation, appoints a subcommittee to determine what approvals the new form should bear. Gray drafts a second suggestion: a form to initiate discontinuance of any form, but on second thought tosses it in the wastebasket.

With all this successfully under way, Brown has a further thought. "Now we are ready for an all-out attack on overhead." Yet another form is released, on which managers must list in order of declining essentiality all the separate functions of their departments and the employee-hours expended on each. Then they are to identify functions that can be eliminated, with attendant savings in overhead. The managers tackle this chore with professional skill. One manager "redundates," as he puts it, a job held by the president's neighbor's daughter. Others list as dispensable those onerous chores that they perform at the behest of sister departments. Still others mark for removal those make-work jobs being done by persons who are about to retire anyway. Out at Deaf Smith, Gray has no problem. He lists as expendable several positions that he had artfully budgeted but never filled. At the end of the program Brown is pleased to tell the board of directors that reorganization has accomplished a 5 percent reduction in the number of positions in the company.

Oddly, the payroll remains relatively unchanged. Brown takes a Draconian measure that he knows has worked elsewhere. "We're going to have a 10 percent across-the-board cut, and I mean heads, not empty jobs! And no department is immune. We've got to get rid of the deadwood! We've got to scrape away the rust! There are too many people here who aren't pulling their weight!" A sad exodus begins. But his vice president of human relations assures him that this time the payroll has indeed been reduced, or rather will be by next year, "After we've got over the hump of separation pay, accumulated vacation and holiday pay, annuity purchases, and our increased unemployment compensation charges. And oh yes, it may be even better than you planned. Some of our people got a little antsy, the way things are going, and have listened to those headhunters. Let's see . . . our chief engineer, our manager of market research, two polymer chemists and two internal auditors, all hard to replace. If, of course, you do want to replace them. Not that it's any problem," he adds hastily. "It's just a matter of agency fees, relocation expense, and perhaps higher salaries to attract the kind of—". Seeing Brown's glare, he bustles from the office.

But now Brown is about to take a giant step. From all sides in the central office he has heard nothing but scorn and contempt for that backward, out-of-date Deaf Smith factory, so miserably run that it sometimes takes up to two weeks to answer a letter; where Buck Gray, that so-called manager, is never even in his office to receive phone calls. ("Probably goofing around on the factory floor to avoid them," says a central office manager.) Brown is convinced that Deaf Smith should be closed down. Isn't that what all other companies are doing, rationalizing and consolidating their facilities? It's got to make sense. He has had a member of the analysis department secretly at work on the project. To his surprise the immediate effect on costs is adverse: those termination expenses, plus the cost of relocating equipment. And then absorbing the Deaf Smith production into the company's remaining factories will mean substituting higher labor rates, to say nothing of more premium second-shift time. And distribution expense may go up a tad. On the other hand, writing off Deaf Smith will effect a reduction in fixed assets and inventories, real balance sheet magic to report to the Board. Says the analyst, "It may not be something that short-term tacticians can appreciate. But for strategists like you who can see down the years, it's a star-fix on our long-term objectives." Brown agrees. "You have to step back in order to leap forward," he says.

But before he can shed Deaf Smith, Brown finds himself stepping not back but out, "to pursue personal interests," the brief press release says. "George was pretty good," says one of the board members to a friend, "and he sure stirred up a storm. The only trouble was it was a dust storm. We needed a rainmaker."

What is wrong here? This company must have had something going for it or it wouldn't have managed to reach its present size. It has products, it has customers, it even (until recently) had net income after taxes. It is peopled with dedicated, competent employees. But it is in trouble.

To Jim Green, Brown's successor, it is obvious that the measures taken so far have been inadequate. The company is as cluttered as a Victorian parlor. You can't make your way through the bric-a-brac. Brown's solution was to empty the ashtrays. Green is thinking of a more thorough attack. This company has got itself so ill-structured that it trips up its own business. It is due for a comprehensive and genuine reorganization.

Many companies are unable to realize their potential because of poor organization. Some clues are:

- Internal bickering, even warfare
- Inability to get anything decided or done
- Failure to follow up on commitments or instructions
- Inaction because of multiplicity of approvals
- Too many decisions going all the way to the top
- Difficulty in pinning down accountability for results
- Actions taken without considering their effect on other parts of business
- Lack of expertise in key areas
- Persistence of outmoded practices because no one has authority to change
- The same functions and records showing up in multiple parts of the organization without overall guidelines or coordination
- Lots of authority but little know-how in key posts
- Excessive overhead
- Insulated "empires"
- Overlapping and contradictory supervision
- Positions with heavy accountability, but inadequate budget
- Management time taken up with things not essential to production, sales, or finances
- No opportunity for creative people to move up
- Slowness in response to market and environmental change (and, in fact, failure to *create* change)

- Domination by one part of business at expense of others
- Sales organization not appropriate to customer alignment
- Product lines not getting focused attention
- And of course, the biggest clues of all: low profitability, falling market share, and declining sales.

Reorganizations are going on all the time. Occasionally, if they are massive, they show up in newspaper stories. When Apple Computer restructured itself in 1985 every financial-page reader learned what had happened. Others, less publicized, are reported only in their incidental effects: the closing of a factory, the opening of a new regional office, the reduction of a headquarters staff, the merging of two companies, the sell-off of another, the addition or dropping of a product line. Many internal reorganizations are never reported at all, but they are nevertheless effective. For companies, reorganizations are almost a form of life process. They are part of growing up.

But though they are not uncommon, they are not uniformly successful in achieving their ends. Some accomplish only internal turmoil. In fact, reorganization can be a cure more painful than the disease. For example, the horrid apprehension that it is about to bring upheavals in the power structure may rocket some good employees right out of the company. For those who stay, the uncertainty as to the safety of their jobs may impair their health and performance. Long-range projects and plans may be interrupted by a "why-bother" attitude.

And once the reorganization is undertaken, further difficulties may vitiate its success. Errors and oversights in the planning of it may wreck new relationships and arrangements. At one company, for example, in eliminating the die-making department, no one has thought to do something about the heat-treating department. What's going to be done with it? Employees in departments new to them have difficulty in establishing new loyalties and relinquishing old ones. A new and unknown boss? A new and suspicious set of subordinates? They have trouble fitting into unfamiliar groups. They pretend to learn the substance and the "feel" of jobs to which they have been reassigned; and go home frightened. A cloud of sorrow over demotions and terminations obscures the pleasures of promotions and retentions. Long-standing personal ties between employees and suppliers and customers are disrupted and the forging of new bonds slows the momentum of the business. The fear of further change pervades the organization. Something has been arbitrarily announced. It does not make any sense. What if the same thing happens again?

Well-meant reorganization, too hastily handled, can turn out to be unintended disorganization.

As a result, a reorganization may endow a company only with a rash of totally unexpected new problems replacing the old. ("Archives? What do I know about who's responsible for archives? I never heard of them." "Well, we seem to have done away with the archives group and now there's a lawyer and three paralegals in the lobby with a court order for our 1978 sales correspondence and no one knows what to tell them.") In the haste to rearrange the organization chart no one has thought out what happens after moving day. Six vice presidents and ten general managers have a rough idea that the company is regrouping, discharged employees are wondering what to tell their families, and those left are searching their desks for Rolaids.

Within the year, the top executive, his ears ringing with up-front and backstairs reports of gum-ups and patch-ups, begins to wonder if a second reorganization is going to be needed to correct the oversights of the first.

It need not be thus. With thoughtful planning and adroit execution a company can replace the ponderous organization that was good enough for yesterday with a new streamlined vehicle engineered for today and maybe even tomorrow. And it can do so with minimum interruption to the business, with invigoration of the personnel, and with favorable long-term effects on the financial numbers. Why bother with it otherwise? Why go through a ceremonial rite of passage without some certainty as to results?

A reorganization that is skillfully rather than carelessly executed is recognized by these characteristics:

- Employees understand what the reorganization consists of.
- Employees accept the need for reorganization.
- Employees realize that in the long run reorganization benefits them by strengthening the company that pays them.
- Reorganization takes place with minimum confusion; everyone knows where they will be and what they will do.
- It does not impede the course of business.
- It accomplishes a quick transition.
- It is sensitive to human feelings.
- It is designed to meet specific objectives.
- It is closely monitored and followed up.
- It creates a favorable impression on outsiders.
- It does not introduce legal problems.
- It is performed at minimum expense.

Helping to assure these results is one aim of this book. Reorganization is a tricky and risky enterprise. In the following chapters we will examine its purposes, methods, and often unforeseen pitfalls. Rather than get into academic organization theory we will concentrate on how-to-do-it approaches. These, though seemingly trivial, may lead to success.

Our scope will be limited. We are not getting into financial restructuring, a speciality in itself. Nor are we covering only minor rearrangements such as a shuffle of vice presidential incumbents or the transfer, for example, of the sales planning department from Marketing to Sales. No, we are talking bigger moves: in a company, a division, a headquarters, a major office or factory. It is in such areas that reorganization is most complex and also, if done well, most rewarding.

Everyone in the company has a feeling that the place could run a little more effectively than it does. If only, they think, remembering the Omar Khayyàm of their teens, they could "shatter it to bits—and then re-mould it nearer to the Heart's Desire!"

For companies must, like Darwin's biota, adapt to their environment if they are to survive. Only "shattering" is not enough. It is the skill in remoulding that produces performance and profits nearer to the heart's desire.

So we are going to look at this remoulding.

2

Why Reorganize?

Let us take "reorganization" to mean any substantial change in the grouping or relationship of people and positions in the company. And when we say "company" let it be understood that much of what we discuss applies as well to universities, hospitals, institutions, and government bodies.

All such groups inevitably experience unplanned reorganization over time. They are like a landscape in which a few trees spring up, a pond dries out, a house appears in the valley, a hillside erodes away; in a few decades the scene is, to the city dweller returning to his childhood home, unrecognizable. Companies also experience a slow metamorphosis, internal empires dissolving with the retirement of an executive, new departments like data processing getting established, some functions (e.g., government relations or auditing) gradually expanding, others (e.g., operations research?) dwindling and being absorbed. Executives and managers come and go, and the company resiliently accommodates to their varying influences. Organizations are always changing, spontaneously and quietly.

IDENTIFY GOALS OF REORGANIZATION

A deliberate major reorganization, on the other hand, is a different matter. It happens all at once. It is not a minor reaction to a small change in the company; it is an attempt to provoke a large change. It is not merely a response, it is a stimulus.

But a stimulus to do what? Anyone embarking on a reorganization must have some end in mind. In fact it is a good idea to set down on paper, right at the very beginning: "The purpose of this reorganization is to accomplish the following results:...." Then at the end of the planning period, and before implementation, this statement can be reviewed to see if what was intended is likely to be realized. Still later, *after* implementation, it can be checked again to see if the change was carried out in a way that really accomplished its purposes. You do not want to start out for Phoenix and find, at the end of your trip, that you are sitting in the airport in Altoona, Pennsylvania. That is what happened to poor George Brown: he set out to reduce paperwork and wound up with a new department.

So reorganization has, of course, purposes. What kind? They are various. Sometimes several different ones are combined in a single shake-up. Sometimes one is a natural fallout of another. Let us look at some examples.

REDUCE CAPITAL ASSETS

A reduction in capital assets may be undertaken to nourish the balance sheet. The company desires, for example, to close down three of its chain of factories and absorb their production in the remaining plants. Foremost to be dealt with, of course, is the *de*organization of the victim factories themselves. But then there is fallout, too. Are as many regional managers of factories still needed? Will the reduction in workload from these deceased factories permit a thinning of head-quarters staff—engineering, quality assurance, accounting, and many others? Will the remaining factories taking over their former sister factories' work require augmentation of personnel? And should a few of the closed factories' most promising staff be reassigned to slots elsewhere? *What* slots?

Sweetening the balance sheet is the destination, but reorganization is the track that gets there.

REDUCE INVENTORIES

Inventory reduction (raw, in-process, and finished goods) is another balance-sheet improvement. Lower inventories means more cash. But how is inventory reduction accomplished? One obvious way is to trim the number of branch warehouses. Like factory closing, this initiates (or should initiate) a train of organization changes elsewhere: in the remaining warehouses now handling a thicker shipping book, in the possible transfers of dejobbed personnel, and in headquarters staff (the central transportation and warehousing departments, for example). A change from private to public warehouses may bring even more sweeping personnel rearrangements. Alternatively, a decision for asset release through mathematical control of inventories to minimum levels (maybe even "just-in-time" delivery) may call for changes in the production scheduling system, supported in turn by reinforced logistics staff. Reorganizationally this is small stuff—except that it may have ramifications in many departments.

REDUCE PAYROLL COSTS

It is a rare newspaper edition that doesn't carry a story about this or that company unloading employees. For example, here the *Wall Street Journal* mentions that U. S. Steel "has more than halved its salaried staff since 1982, eliminating 16,500 jobs."[1] The line appears near the end of a story, scarcely even news. Such deeds may be done as a cost-cutting move or simply because not enough sales order forms are being filled out (a kind of paperwork reduction that even George Brown would not have welcomed). And the cost cutting may be unavoidable because of faltering profits. Commodore International Ltd., a maker of home computers, had to announce the layoff of 700 employees, or 15 percent of its work force. Why? Because it faced a fourth quarter (1985) loss of $80 million, including a $50 million after-tax writedown of slow-selling inventory. No orders. Even in a profitable company the CEO may feel that force reduction is the thing to do. Everybody is doing it, his consultants tell him.

Even unions do it to their own employees. "USW President Lloyd McBride . . . said the union would reduce its clerical and support staff to about 1,200 employees, a drop of about 200," says another newspaper story.[2]

In any case, such payroll paring may not of itself necessitate reorganization; the organization chart still looks the same, it just has fewer names on it. When, however, there is excision or combination of departments (we will have a lot to say about this later on) the chart undergoes a desirable condensation.

Whatever the primary reason, force reduction needs careful planning. You cannot just line up the troops and command: "Every tenth person step forward." You have to decide who's to go, and who's to tell them, and who's to pick up whatever they've been doing (which we will also come to later on).

Usually force reduction has a monetary goal: so many dollars to be saved after termination expenses. This in turn is translated into a number of equivalent employee releases. In estimating the savings, the thing to remember is that more than mere payroll and fringes are affected. Fewer employees also means fewer desks and offices to be cleaned, less travel expense, lower phone bills, utilities savings, and rental reduction on equipment and space. In some instances combination of departments may have ripple effects in other areas: less work for the duplicating or data-entry departments, for example. Taking all these into account may permit dollar-goal attainment with fewer terminations and more modest reorganization than simple pay-check calculations would suggest.

OCCUPY NEW QUARTERS

Sometimes an office move entails a personnel rationalization. For example, a move to smaller quarters may require some tightening up of the employee population. Holding the top staff at a prestige address while shifting the nether ranks to comfortable "back-room" space in a low-rent area may introduce new functional groupings and lines of communication and authority.

AVOID NEW INVESTMENT

Sometimes reorganization offers an opportunity to bypass investment in new facilities. A few examples:

- One of Company A's subsidiaries needs a new factory in the northwest to supply a rising sales curve. Rather than build, the company combines this subsidiary with another capable of handling additional production, thus effecting a reorganization of both into one.
- Company B, rather than build new facilities, acquires a bargain company having spare capacity. Integrative reorganization of both follows.
- The boom in sales of Company C, a mail-order house, is going to require moving to, and equipping, larger quarters. Instead Company C switches to round-the-clock office operation, introducing new supervisory and support organization.
- Company D, rather than put money into new data-processing equipment, turns the whole operation over to an outside service bureau. A network of internal changes in organization is activated.

These are just examples of avoidable investments, seemingly essential, that are really dictated by inflexible organization rather than by physical need. And they can arise in both factory and office.

MAKE-OR-BUY

The make-or-buy decision, when done on a large scale, can have protean effects on the organization. Swinging to "make" increases the demand for internal manpower, perhaps the introduction of new departments, nodes of responsibility, and lines of authority. Focusing on "buy" has an opposite impact. Organizationally it is important to shape the organization to accommodate these changes. In fact, they should be part of the make/buy decision itself, which should not be based on elementary comparisons of buying price vs. manufacturing cost as read from the accounting records. Often enough the gain or loss of in-house factory production resonates in many parts of the company, from power plant to receiving dock to office accounting. Make-or-buy decisions should always consider the gain or loss from organizational adjustment to change.

Potential impact on organizational change is not always readily apparent. Circumstances vary. A movement from make to buy, or vice versa, may be like the slow imperceptible movement of a tide. After a protracted period it leaves some organizational areas stranded but still existent (an in-house foundry, for example) or others inundated and unable to cope with new demands (a receiving or even purchasing department, for example). As a result the need for reorganization to reflect a new manufacturing policy, peeling off or sticking together some departments, strengthening others, may be overlooked. But it will still have to be attended to.

A major, one-time make/buy change in policy should almost immediately modify the appearance of the chart.

SPEED UP REACTION TIME

At the checkout counter in some stores you wait and wait and wait while the clerk punches the sale into a keyboard and a computer whirrs, chatters, and pops before finally issuing a ticket and opening the cash drawer. In others the clerk simply rings up the sale, gives you your change and you're out. The first type has a slow reaction time for its own internal satisfactions; the second gets the whole transaction done quickly. Some companies are like the first. If a competitor comes out with a new package, they take two years before getting a rival one on the shelf. Their internal reaction time is too slow. Restructuring is one way of speeding things up. It does so by changing the ways of doing things.

For example, suppose that a product price change has to pass over fifteen desks for approval before it reaches the field salesperson. That change will be doing well if it gets out in a month. Any reorganization that devises fewer way stations will put the company in closer touch with its customers.

Merely speeding things up is a primary aim of many reorganizations that flatten the company pyramid, pull out multiple levels of supervision, assign decision making (aided by clear policies) to the lowest possible levels, and decentralize to create smaller information loops. George Brown's company in our introductory example presented an organization so finely subdivided that communication could flow within it forever, like electric current in a cryogenic circuit.

FREE UP MANAGEMENT

"I'm like the old woman who lived in a shoe," one president complains. "I've got so many subordinates I don't know what to do." Reporting to him are, in addition to administrative assistants, executives or managers separately in charge of:

Accounting

Auditing

Research

Engineering and Design

Quality Control

Marketing

Sales

European Business

Asian Business

Latin and South American Business

Law

Public Relations

Industrial Relations

Human Resources

Security

Manufacturing

Purchasing

Distribution

Three separate subsidiaries.

He must additionally attend to financial writers, analysts, consultants, newspaper editors, angry consumers, politicians, community leaders, major customers, principal stockholders, bankers, and the board of directors. It is seldom that his anteroom does not harbor at least one fund raiser, protest group, or visiting delegation from overseas. "What," muses his wife, "if there were a mad bomber out there?" "Sometimes I wish there were," he says.

In the meantime a mournful chorus rises from levels below him: "We can't get enough of his time! He won't make decisions! He keeps putting us off!"

Does this company need rewiring from the top down? Yes, it does. Management must free itself to manage.

CLARIFY ACCOUNTABILITIES

"I asked to see whoever was in charge of inventory control," one president laughed, "and fourteen people came into my office!"

Tangled accountabilities often have their roots in the past. For example, in a small family-owned company, everybody meddles in everything and everything gets done. The company grows, and a general diffusion of authority persists. But as departments aggregate together and as new ones are from time to time added, there comes a point when either nothing or too much gets done. Questions and disputes arise: Who buys trucks, the purchasing department or the transportation department? How many different people are signing leases? Who has authority to engage a lawyer? Who is ultimately accountable for security of the company jet? Who is accountable for keeping inventories low?

Clarifying accountabilities often involves changing and regrouping individual positions, a form of reorganization that must be handled with great sensitivity, as though one were assigning all the neighborhood children to different parents.

INTRODUCE PARTICIPATIVE MANAGEMENT

Some authorities recommend relaxing the organization as a means of improving either the quality of work life or the profits, depending on whom they are talking to. I mention this only in passing, for it is not only a large subject but a nebulous one. Companies convinced that overbureaucratic rigidity is bottling up employees' contribution try to loosen up the flow of ideas and initiatives by unlacing the structure.

For them simple bureaucracy does not meet the whole needs of a developing organization. Being, by definition, rigid, it is unable to change itself. It does not accommodate readily to new and special situations. Nor does its stratified hierarchy permit free use of lower-echelon abilities. For these reasons, progressive companies are exploring organizational activity that goes beyond bureaucracy and formal structures. This adaptive, situational type of organization is designed to meet the challenge of a changing economy and society. "Effective organizational units operating in stable parts of the (company) environment are more highly structural, while those in more dynamic parts are less formal.... Communication between people of different ranks tends to resemble lateral consultation rather than vertical command."[3] With such an approach there is less need for people to rely on rank, title, and "authority" as instruments of influence. Yet at the same time, accountabilities must be ever more fully emphasized. This is the challenge of a developing organization: to create liberty and freedom throughout a structure that preserves guarantees to the company of identified, ongoing accountabilities in every function, department, and position. Obviously such a structural change can only be accomplished through a revolution in company psychology.

Since this book is concerned with *re-* rather than *de*organization, the subject is worth noticing, but far beyond our present scope.

INTEGRATE AN ACQUISITION

Bringing two or more companies together is certain to raise organization issues.

In the case of a large company acquiring a small one it may be thought that after a few executive rearrangements and the institution of general controls the small one can be left to run as before, though with greater financial resources to draw on. It doesn't always work out that way, for new constraints enter the picture. Some small companies get away with a lot of things that big ones cannot. Once under the big top their accounting, pricing, ethical practices, waste discharge, plant safety, union (if any) negotiations, and pension plan are going to come under closer scrutiny. Also, there will be opportunities too good to ignore: joint shipping and warehousing, mutual sales personnel, mass buying economies, merger of computing facilities, more highly skilled marketing and engineering, perhaps even absorption of manufacturing into the acquirer's premises. So reorganization gets under way to set up new responsibilities, accountabilities, and authority. When the internal climates of the two companies turn out to be incompatible, further changes may be expected, including employee departures. These in turn open up possibilities for moving or restructuring the positions vacated.

If the acquired company is large, it may conceivably be left to run on its own, connected to its parent only by an umbilicus of dollars. And yet, such are the pressures for generating cash to support the costs of acquisition that upper-level desire for change is to be expected.

Reorganization for any of various reasons must lie uppermost in the mind of anyone planning an acquisition or merger.

DISPOSE OF A SUBSIDIARY

Companies, not always conglomerates, now and then lop off one of their parts in order to get rid of a loser, cure an organizational headache, lay hands on some cash, get out of problem markets, concentrate on one line of business, or meet an antitrust requirement. Once the negotiations are concluded and the papers signed, doing so should merely mean drawing a big X over a wing of the organization chart. But in companies with substantial headquarters staff nothing is this easy. Such staff will undoubtedly have had a vascular connection with the severed member. Now that that member is gone from the body is it not reasonable, nay, mandatory, that there be some corresponding shrinkage in the staff itself? Well, it may be said, nothing to that: just cut out a few jobs. But *what* jobs? And how do you save one-tenth of a one-person incumbency (say, the receptionist) or tolerate what turns out to be a one or two person department? What do you do about 15,000 square feet of variously scattered office space no longer needed? Selloffs mediate, as the scientists say, reorganization of what is left. Or should.

EXPLOIT OUTSIDE SERVICES

Companies do not have to be entirely self-contained. They aren't medieval fortresses. Often functions inserted into the company for the best of reasons years ago can be turned over to outsiders with consequent advantages: savings of space, personnel, inventory, and managerial attention; and at the same time gains from someone else's expertise, versatility, investment, up-to-date facilities, and competitive pricing. From art work and duplicating to lab tests and data processing there is a wide range of outside services readily available, sometimes less expensive because better managed and heavier loaded, waiting to supplant in-house ones. If such services are released from the company drop by drop, any reorganization is apt to be minor. But if there is a general all-at-once housecleaning of the antique organizational furniture, extensive regrouping on the chart must be seriously considered.

PREPARE FOR FUTURE GROWTH

Executives who combine vision with confidence deliberately reshape today's organization to handle tomorrow's growth. They separate out departments that will grow into divisions. They isolate geographic centers that later will become regions. They seed venture units meant to turn into subsidiaries. These and many other organizational changes, quietly carried out, prepare the company to deal with the demands of growth when it comes.

INTRODUCE NEW TECHNOLOGY

Reorganization may be a natural response to new technology. Electronic data processing, with its elimination of many manual functions, is one of the most outstanding examples of this type of change. It has infiltrated every part of business, changing how things are done, where they are done, by whom they are done. Similarly, spreading automation can revise the supervisory assignments in a factory. Adaptation to new chemistry or new inventions can call for expansion of some factory departments, contraction of others; and if it is reflected in new or greater sales, it may entail change in marketing and sales groups as well. Some companies respond to such advances with automatic, ad hoc twitches of their structure. Others manage a planned accommodation to new technology that promptly gets rid of outmoded, superfluous positions while at the same time adequately placing and staffing new groups to exploit new opportunities.

REDUCE VULNERABILITY

To the psychologists' fight/flight responses to danger we may add a third: adapt. What are typical threats, real or anticipated, that can be met by internal adaptation? Some examples are:

- major lawsuits
- product callback
- declining quality
- embezzlement
- government actions or penalties
- loss of market share.

Defenses vary with the cause. For example, again:

- Replace internal weak spots where short-sightedness or resistance to whistle-blowers has exposed the company to lawsuits.
- Strengthen or elevate certain functions. In the face of callbacks and declining quality, for example, reposition the quality control function for greater authority.
- Separate functions to provide more checks and balances (against, for example, embezzlement).
- Install in-house expertise and especially, authority (to deal with governmental problems, for example).
- Overhaul marketing and sales or perhaps strengthen the product design function to recapture market share.

While these may range from trivial to widespread reassignments they have one thing in common. Whatever has gone wrong and must now be corrected, someone in the company probably saw it coming but was not in a position to take preventive action. Counsel: reorganize.

CONVERT THRESHOLD COMPANY

There comes a time when a growing owner- or family-operated company must cross a line. It introduces professional management. It focuses accountabilities. It subdivides its undifferentiated mass into formal departments. It organizes. And then, likely as not, it will suffer internal feuding until subsequent reorganization, something like the discard and draw in a game of gin, gives it a game-winning hand.

CONSOLIDATE FUNCTIONS

Frequently reorganization occurs in order to permit a consolidation of functions in the interests of economy and efficient management. For example, an item in the *Wall Street Journal* reads: "Phillips Petroleum Co. . . . is eliminating five executive positions through attrition and merging two units as the latest step in its restructuring plan. Phillips said yesterday that it will combine the petroleum-product and chemical operations into a single unit because the two units require similar feedstocks and because there are duplicate staff and support positions."[4]

Function-marriage carries a number of benefits. The Lockheed Corporation consolidated twenty-four different line and staff functions into four groups. "The spokesman for the company said in an interview that Roy A. Anderson, the chairman and chief executive officer, and L. O. Kitchen, the president and chief operating officer, had found it difficult to keep track of the operating companies." Moreover, "putting the different organizations into groups would also help bring workers into closer contact with each other, across current lines of organization. . . . It would also enable the company to focus its projects better and allocate resources more efficiently."[5]   Such combinings originate a new alignment of jobs and also an expulsion of no longer necessary ones (in Phillips' case, redundant employees were transferred to vacancies in other departments, the company said).

CHANGE COMMAND

Change of command at the top often induces further changes just below. For example, when Marshall Smith replaced Jack Tramiel as president of Commodore International Ltd., he brought a 180-degree change in management style. It was reported in the *Wall Street Journal* that "months of infighting and indecision resulted," and Smith found it necessary to hire "a cadre of technology and marketing executives from PepsiCo Inc., Apple, Nabisco Brands, Inc. and IBM."[6] This is not unusual. A new president wants to introduce his own ways of doing things, and the inherited phalanx of under-executives have dug in their heels. Simple solution: bring in new executives who can share and fulfill the president's intentions. But these recruits encounter below them the same problem he did. And they know a few good people on the outside who are both bright and committed to their management style. And these people, once brought aboard, begin realigning.... A cascade of reorganization pours down through the company. Unless it is recognized for what it is and well coordinated, it can soon have everybody at sixes and sevens.

Command change does not always start at the very peak of the pyramid. It may occur down inside too. A manager or executive is about to leave the ranks—perhaps fired, perhaps retired. His or her successor may have a different mix of experience and talents. Reorganization may occur to achieve a good fit between the person and the job. For example, if an outsider hired for the position of operations vice president has a strong background in warehousing and transportation, these functions might be moved from the sales division to Operations to get the advantage of new thinking. Undoubtedly the newcomer will also initiate one of those cascades of further change mentioned above.

EXTEND BUSINESS

Plans to extend the business often depend on a preliminary realignment of positions. As examples of business reorientation:

- Change markets from wholesalers or distributors to retailers or ultimate consumers—may require starting up specialist groups in the sales, marketing, packaging, and physical distribution departments.

- Introduce new product lines—may support new elements all through the company, in product management, manufacturing, engineering, package and product design, quality control, and production and inventory management. If product lines are dropped, the reverse effect should not be overlooked.

- Improve customer service—may call for new responsibilities, possibly new or changed positions, in sales, broker management, manufacturing, physical distribution, and even accounts receivable.

Only confusion and low goal attainment can flow from major business changes unaccompanied by attention to the relationships and assignments of the positions that are to accomplish them. A common complaint: "How can I get this done with no more time, no more authority, and no more personnel?"

CHANGE PRODUCT/FUNCTION EMPHASIS

Some companies are organized by function—marketing, accounting, engineering, research, and logistics, for example are performed by unified groups providing their service to all products.

Others are product-segregated. Each major division handles a group of related products and carries its own crew of product managers, accountants, engineers, research scientists/technologists, and logistics coordinators. As a variant on product orientation, a company may split its subdivisions according to market. A food manufacturer, for example, has one group of salespersons and product managers addressing the retail market, another the foodservice market. An electrical equipment manufacturer splits its operations into those serving the government market, the utilities market, and the construction market.

The advantages of the functional arrangement are high-level professionalism and clear-cut career paths, avoidance of duplication, and uniformity of approach. The disadvantages: narrow-gauge managers, shallow knowledge of any one product, diffusion of effort, priority rankings that never reach some products, and emphasis on professional rather than product requirements.

The advantages of product orientation are total dedication to getting each product made and sold, team cooperation, great depth of product knowledge, assurance that necessary efforts will not be subordinated to the needs of other products, development of broad-scale manageriality and entrepreneurship, and for the future, preparation for divestment or subsidiary-ing. Additionally, the narrowing of job horizons means that employees have to deal with less information, which in turn improves accuracy and reaction time. The disadvantages: duplication of function on a company-wide basis (not entirely an evil), growth of variant procedures, competition for still-functional services (e.g., distribution), and relatively lower-level dead-end jobs, especially for professionals.

A further possible disadvantage is the need for continued oversight from a headquarters staff. If each product division has its own controller, for instance, a corporate controller must still coordinate budgets and procedures. These overlaps seem like an extra cost, particularly if not considered in conjunction with the offsetting, increased profitability of product divisionality.

Because of these trade-offs of good and bad it is not uncommon for companies to switch from one to the other, somewhat like the reversals in polarity of the Earth. When this happens the reorganizations are complex indeed and it is safe to say that in no case are they accompanied by work force enlargement. For example, in 1985 Apple Computer Inc. underwent, according to the *Wall Street Journal*, a "major reorganization aimed at lowering costs and restoring some stability to the company.... The restructuring splits Apple into two functional groups and dissolves its two product-oriented divisions. The company's new operations group will oversee manufacturing and distribution ... along with product development. Marketing and sales will be overseen by the second group.... The changes are expected to lessen the intense rivalry between the product divisions and help trim costs."[7] Shortly afterward Apple announced that it was closing some factories, shifting production to others, and laying off 1,200 employees. Change in orientation almost guarantees change in organization.

CHANGE GEOGRAPHIC GROUPINGS

Setting up a west (or east) coast division, reconfiguring sales regions and territories, establishing ultranational divisions or subsidiaries—all these geographic tectonics are undertaken to enhance revenues and, it is hoped, net income after tax. They can be realized only through new organizational geometry. For example, International Business Machines Corporation split its sales force into two groups: one to handle all customers in the Northeast and Middle West, and another to handle those in the South and West. The purpose was to move decision making down the line to give sales managers more flexibility in deploying their resources.

CENTRALIZE/DECENTRALIZE

What do we mean by "centralized?" Though usually applied to an organization having multiple major components, it may have various connotations; an organization may be centralized or decentralized with respect to geography, management, or staff.

For example, consider a university. On its campus it has several colleges. These are geographically centralized. Elsewhere in the city and in nearby towns it has additional campuses. These are geographically decentralized.

If the university chancellor gives heavy direction on decisions and actions to the head of each college or campus, the organization is managerially centralized. If the local heads operate fairly autonomously, being guided only by policies, budgets, and long-range plans, the management is decentralized.

If the university provides from its headquarters to the component colleges and campuses staff such services as personnel management, payroll, purchasing, and administrative data processing, it is staff-centralized. If it has a skeleton staff at headquarters dispensing minimum overall guidance and coordination to local staffs, it is staff-decentralized.

It is the same way with companies, and they have their problems. Some are all in one place and are thinking of branching out. Some are already dispersed and are thinking of contracting.

Generally speaking, centralizing has its advantages. For example:

- Avoidance of staff duplication: a single headquarters staff may be smaller than a multitude of local staffs. Also, it may be able to afford a level of professionalism that scattered localities cannot, which may be directly reflected in profit-making performance throughout the company.
- Quality of personnel: it is easier to attract top graduates to a headquarters city than to stick them in isolated cabbage patches. Moreover, high-level professionals—accountants, engineers, scientists, and the like may be affordable only when serving company-wide needs.
- Uniformity: for the company's own protection it may be necessary to delimit local authority in many matters relating to law, policy, union negotiation, variations in formula or design, and procedures for bookkeeping, product inspection, purchasing, and data processing.
- Economy: doing everything in a single office or factory (as compared with several) may provide economies of staff, supervision, fuel, space, taxes, equipment and mass purchasing that offset greater transportation and labor costs. And maybe not: it all depends on the company.

Decentralizing, too, has its merits.

- Better customer service: local installations permit prompter, more attentive coordination with customers' needs.
- Faster response time: things get done more quickly if handled on the spot rather than through a bureaucracy (as Buck Gray knew).
- Managerial grooming: in a decentralized company with local autonomy, managers gain experience in decision making and tradeoffs as preparation for future promotion.
- Economy: again, this depends on the company, but in some cases labor rates and transportation costs are held to a minimum by geographically decentralizing factories and warehouses.
- Necessity: McDonald's cannot have one giant hamburger outlet per city. They have to put individual stores where the traffic is.

From this it is seen that various combinations are possible: centralized or decentralized facilities, and/or management, and/or staff services. Sometimes companies that have succeeded with one alternative discover good reasons for changing. For example, a jump in transportation expenses may dictate going from central to regional warehousing; conversely, new communication and data processing equipment may render dispersed order-entry offices unnecessary.

Consider IBM, which developed its personal computer in a decentralized location, Florida. Once the PC was successful, IBM in what was surely an odd decision for a company that extols electronic communications as a replacement for personal confrontation, announced that it was going to move the personal-computer division headquarters to New Jersey, "so that," according to the *Wall Street Journal*, "the once-independent unit can better work with other IBM divisions. The move will affect the 200-member headquarters staff of IBM's Entry Systems division."[8]

Some companies are both centralized and decentralized. General Nutrition Corporation, for example, runs a large mail-order business from one location, but it also sets up retail health food stores in shopping centers all over the country.

It is almost axiomatic that a change in organization must accompany any change to or from centralization.

BREAK UP CLIQUES

It occasionally happens that a company finds its most enthusiastic competition occurring, not with its outside rivals, but among cliques and groups within it. Manufacturing is at perpetual war with Quality Control. Sales hates to carry out Marketing's plans. Engineering ignores all suggestions from Research. The machining department blames all its problems on the foundry. The receiving inspectors scheme to reject what Purchasing has ordered in. The cotton buyer will not talk to the spinning department. The safety manager's secretary will not talk to the environmental manager's secretary. The company is fragmented into cliques.

One way to bring peace is to call in organizational development experts to achieve company-wide consensus on rights and expectations. Another method, often used, is disemployment. Duchies are broken up and redistributed. Uncooperative satraps are removed from their provinces. It is not the structure that needs reorganizing, it is the people in it.

Even when things seem to be going well, with managers competently (albeit jealously) on top of their domains and everything running as smoothly as quartz clockwork, there is something to be said for a game of managerial musical chairs. It breaks up complacency. Managers who have migrated from one department to another find themselves in strange territory. In the new department they have no commitment to past practices. Everything is up for question. Good employees and good ideas that somehow got overlooked in the past get a fresh inspection. The transferred managers are no longer coasting along on the smooth highway of routine, they are hacking their way through a jungle and they want to come up with a treasure-find or two, to demonstrate their genius (and perhaps also expose what their predecessor missed). Even seemingly capricious reorganization is not without its virtues.

PREPARE NEW TALENT

Some reorganization is done in the interests of developing human resources. For example:

- Data Processing is moved from the administration division to the controller's in order to give the controller experience with management of this activity.
- Sales Planning is moved from Marketing to Sales so that its head will be more adaptable to both environments.
- Engineering and Purchasing are put under the vice president of manufacturing in order to give that executive more experience in managing tradeoffs of objectives.
- The vice president of manufacturing and the vice president of sales are interchanged on their jobs, seeming misfits both, to broaden their background as candidates for promotion to the next level up.
- Several departments are rearranged in order to provide lower-level managerial training and testing for promising young newcomers.

Though on the face of it these moves seem to involve only a few people, they will probably lead to further, more extensive ones. Newly appointed executives and managers often initiate changes in the personnel and structure under them in order to get the machine in condition for their style of driving.

SUMMARY

Reorganization is a broad term. It may include such forms as:

- Keep the structure, shuffle the people.
- Keep the structure, reduce the number of people.
- Change the structure, shuffle positions, keep the people.

- Pare (or consolidate) the structure, reduce the number of people.
- Enlarge the structure, add people.
- Combine structures and keep some people (as with an acquisition).

Whatever its nature, it is done purposefully. Often one reorganization meets several of the objectives described on the preceding pages. But purpose is easy to lose sight of. Reorganization gone amok can itself become the primary goal, just as getting the carpenters, electricians, and plumbers all scheduled and active at the right time can come to seem like the most important goal of remodeling a house. But it isn't. How you live during and after the remodeling is what counts.

Reorganization has its unpleasant aspects: firing people; demoting them; staffing them under unfamiliar bosses; promoting them to scary new responsibilities; breaking up happy groups; moving families to strange cities; moving employees, for that matter, to strange offices. But these are only interim effects.

Once a reorganization is successfully completed, the company should be a far better place to work. Old frustrations have been eliminated, more profits are in the offing, many employees have better, more challenging, more interesting jobs, the whole place runs more smoothly.

These ends are attainable only, however, if the reorganization process itself is well thought out. An ill-planned one can impose, after the trauma of change, further agony yet. People are not clear about whom they are to report to and what they are to do. They are unsure about the effect on their pay. Some, handled too roughly, propagate gripes or rumors. Customers and suppliers discover themselves facing an impenetrable thicket. Trying to remedy this confusion and turmoil diverts the company from the very ends it has pursued.

No matter how worthy the intentions, the transition phases of reorganization are an uncertain bridge. The president thinks he is crossing the Rubicon, the employees wonder if they are not crossing the Styx. But if things turn out right the company is crossing the Jordan, and on the other side lie the rewards of a journey well taken.

How can a company be reengineered so as to assure these rewards? By following three familiar imperatives: plan, execute, follow-up. Why, there is nothing to it . . . or is there?

NOTES

1. *Wall Street Journal*, 11 July 1985.
2. *Wall Street Journal*, 17 Dec. 1982.

3. Paul Lawrence and Jay Lorsch, *Organization and Environment* (Homewood, Ill.: Richard D. Irwin, Inc., 1969).

4. *Wall Street Journal*, 10 July 1985.

5. *New York Times*, 6 Apr. 1983.

6. *Wall Street Journal*, 19 July 1985.

7. *Wall Street Journal*, 3 June 1985.

8. *Wall Street Journal*, 14 June 1985.

Getting Started

You can, of course, conduct a reorganization with very little planning at all. Just decide what is to be done, tell everyone concerned, and let them work out the details themselves. How do you tell them? Well, just post a notice on the bulletin boards. Or you could call a meeting of the employees affected, announce the changes, throw a new organization chart on the screen, and then dismiss the meeting. Mission accomplished. No need to over-explain. You are running things, not them. Let them get back to their work. If some of them realize, as they stumble from the auditorium, that they do not have any work to get back to, they can go to a personnel clerk who has an envelope with their name on it containing all the farewell provisions. And if the remaining ones, who have been variously promoted, demoted, transferred, or ignored, do not know what to do next, let them work it out. For what they are getting paid they ought to have enough brains to do that. What comes first in the business is business, not a lot of rumor and gossip and wasted time on reorganization. Except . . . .

The main purpose of reorganizing is to make the business run better. Right? And it is the employees who keep the business running. Right? And the more thoroughly they understand what they are doing, the better they will do it. Right? And the better their emotional tone the better they will understand. Right? And the better you manage the reorganization and control its outcome, the better their understanding and emotional tone. Right? So what you ought to do instead of posting that notice or calling that meeting, is hand out at quitting time on Friday a ten-page bulletin describing all the moves in detail so everyone learns them fully (and on their own time). Right? Well, maybe not.

We are going to consider alternative ways of conducting a reorganization. They may seem a little detailed and time-consuming. But why not? When you think of the number of hours and drawings that Engineering, say, puts into designing and installing the new energy-conserving equipment, isn't the design of the company itself worth equally painstaking investment? Shouldn't it be just as thoughtfully planned and executed? So if your first decision was "reorganize" your second should be "do it well". Doing it well requires a sequence of steps that we'll now examine.

DEFINE THE OBJECTIVES

The first step is to define what the reorganization is aimed at. Frequently it is one or more of the good things mentioned in Chapter 2—plus others peculiar to the case at hand ("create a place at the top for my son-in-law").

The object of the change should, as mentioned before, be written for future guidance. "The purpose of this reorganization is to accomplish the following results:...." Some elementary care is advisable in committing the objective to writing. "Clear out the top deck of old, stick-in-the-mud employees," for example, is not a recommended statement to go into the record for future paralegals to find. It should not say "old."

After planning gets under way additional objectives may appear to be realizable, and they should be retroactively added to the original statement.

DESCRIBE THE NATURE OF THE CHANGE

The next step is to outline the specific moves contemplated. Some of these will deal with divisions and departments. For example:

- Combine divisions so that no more than the following six functions report directly to the president: Marketing and Sales, Operations, Finance, Law, Quality and Research, Administration.
- Create a product-oriented structure with the following principal divisions: white goods, home appliances, shop appliances, industrial hardware.
- Realign Research and Quality into separate departments, with Research coming under a new division, Research and Engineering.
- Replace the following departments with outside suppliers....

Others may deal with positions and individuals:

- Eliminate all 'Assistant Manager' positions.

- Have all factory controllers report to the headquarters controller instead of to the factory managers.

- Remove 1,200 employees from the salaried payroll.

- Effect transfers in order to expose the following individuals to more comprehensive company experience....

ASSIGN THE JOB

Now the reorganization must be worked out in detail. Who is going to work it out? More is required, as we shall see, then just drawing a few boxes on a piece of paper. New titles must sometimes be assigned. People must be chosen for the boxes. Spots (maybe nowhere) must be found for displaced persons. At least synopsis job descriptions are helpful. Proposed salary arrangements ought to be worked out. Costs (or savings) of the change should be estimated. And everyone involved must be notified.

What kind of person can work out the details, not just of laying out the reorganization scheme but also of implementing it? Let us take the worst (that is, the toughest) case, a company-wide regrouping of divisions and departments, with creation and abandonment of many individual positions and a substantial cut in the personnel roster. Except in a very small company this is not something to be worked out by the president nor yet, in all likelihood, by the vice presidents. There is too much full-time detail in it. Yet it takes someone with an intimate knowledge of everything that goes on in the company, plus some ability to visualize new ways of doing things, plus an inborn propensity for keeping the mouth shut about confidential information.

The personnel department is the obvious choice for candidates; but there are usually a few other sources. Systems analysts, industrial engineers, and internal auditors often have extensive knowledge of what is going on and are particularly likely to be conscious of overstaffed or redundant activities that no one else has paid attention to.

How many people are needed? It depends on the extent of the reorganization. A very small-scope shift—say, interchanging two vice presidents or combining the duplicating department with the mailroom—can be handled directly by the person responsible for it. But even limited moves—the vice presidential one, for example—may, as we have seen, set off bigger ones. The president hiccups one small change and the whole company goes into a convulsion. Who is to work out all the details then? Working up a proposal may be a one-person job, provided that person has access to job descriptions and confidential secretarial service. Or it may be a task force undertaking, the force consisting of executives who meet with the "gofer." Or—far out!—it may be a consensus group of lower-level employees, who ideate the outrageous, and democratically shape the organization they belong to. Not to be sour about a well-meaning approach, this process is apt to take more time than any other, and in the end deliver the wishes of the most dominant, though not necessarily the brightest, group member. But it is a possibility.

In any case, the undertaking is assigned, accompanied by a statement of mission; for example, "Devise a new organization that will meet the stated objectives. Devise a plan for introducing, carrying out, and following up on this reorganization. Manage, directly or indirectly, all elements of this change for a smooth and effective transition." The person(s) assigned will be expected to:

- Lay out a working schedule
- Submit a preliminary proposal
- Meet a deadline for the final proposal
- Implement (with help as necessary) the approved proposal
- Document the progress of the job
- Report back if any problems arise
- Provide progress reports at specified times.

In turn they are granted access to:

- Necessary private work space and secretarial help
- Job descriptions and evaluations
- Existing organization charts and personnel rosters
- Appraisals of individual performance
- Short- and long-range strategic business plans
- Company and departmental budgets
- The initiator of the project for consultation at any time.

They should also receive specific input on guidelines and policies governing the change. They may, in fact, present for approval by the Initiator a proposed set of policies derived from company experience, previous discussions, and a knowledge of what is apt to be needed.

Such policies are essential to keep the reorganization from going in a different direction from what is expected, and they cover a lot of ground.

Before getting into them I would like, for ease in future reading, to define a couple of terms. Whoever is charged with working out the details of the reorganization, whether one person or a task force, I will refer to as the Planner. Whoever the Planner reports to on this special assignment—the president (or better yet, the president and a team of vice presidents, excluding of course, any vulnerable members) or a division or department head—I will call the Initiator.

DETERMINE POLICIES

Both in planning and execution decision points arise. Some of them bear on the reorganization process itself, others concern its effect on employees. How are these decisions to be addressed? Having guidelines—rules or policies—in place from the start helps ensure consistency, fairness, and acceptability to both the company and its constituent workforce. It keeps the machine rolling smoothly from start to finish.

One of the first things the Planner should do is set down a list of policy statements. These are the fence that separates how things will be done in this particular reorganization, in this particular company, at this particular time, from a wilderness of alternatives.

"Well," it may be said, "we already have a company policy book and we have well-understood company practices." Fine! That makes it easier. But all the same, a list of policies guiding the forthcoming upheaval is still useful. The reorganization is a special case, not day-to-day business. Presenting its own problems, it may need its own rules. Indeed, the opportunity to cut loose old policies that have been tying the company down may be one of its virtues.

Having assembled major policies to answer any "how" questions, the Planner reviews them with the Initiator to be sure everyone is on the same track. Perhaps some proposed policies get changed. That is why they are taken up for review.

After this preparatory tuning, the Planner can get going equipped with pre-set policy decisions to guide him. What should these policies cover?

SPACING

Is the reorganization to be accomplished in one (ideally not too fell) swoop or is it to occur in a sequence of steps? The sequence solution has two possible rationales:

1. To keep the change within doable bounds. For example, if the marketing and sales divisions are each to be reorganized, it may be easier for all concerned if Marketing, say, is restructured first and then Sales later on. If a group of factories is to be closed with some employees, facilities, and

production being moved to others, a one-at-a-time schedule may be more readily handled.

2. To set up interim changes that prepare the ground for subsequent ones. For example, product groups in Marketing may be restructured to give more independence to new product lines, which may in turn form the nucleus for new businesses to be organized later on. Or a number of departments in a factory—say, pattern-making, casting, forging, and extrusion departments—may be replaced by outside services as a prelude to consolidation of the remaining departments six months later.

The guidelines should therefore rule from the start whether the reorganization is to be revealed all at once like a diorama or bit-by-bit like a slide show.

CONFIDENTIALITY

A primary question to be decided is: How much are we going to let out about what is being planned here? Well, it all depends.

In some cases a frank announcement can be made: "We are studying ways of being better organized to meet our business challenges." If the company climate is generally good, if the profit picture is favorable, if the employees are by and large satisfied and competent, such openness carries little risk. In fact, if the reorganization is one of expansion, it is all to the good.

But suppose it is the other way around: everyone knows the company is losing money, sales are down, and there is not enough work to keep people busy. Or suppose it is a company so riddled with internal feuding that obviously there are going to be big winners and big losers in any shake-up. An up-front announcement can frighteningly bring right under their eyeballs what everybody had hoped was a distant judgment day. Unpleasant reactions ensue. Whispering sessions form at the copying machines; work assignments lose immediacy; the real pessimists start taking home tools, stationery, and confidential files; the high caliber employees jot down the phone numbers of headhunters; the low caliber ones step up their Valium intake; and the on-premises drug dealer makes extra trips to the bank.

Rather than make any announcement at all, a company may therefore decide to keep the whole planning process under wraps until ready to put it into effect. This is not too hard to do if only one or two trustworthy people are in on it. But if various supervisors must be contacted from time to time for information, the secret is bound to leak out. It will get around the company that an earthquake is approaching. The anxiety meter will go up a notch.

This may not be all bad. In some companies rumor is part of the daily meat and drink. So here's today's rumor: who's excited? And you might also contend that an event for which people have been gently prepared by the rumor mill is less devastating than one that drops on their heads like the Siberian meteorite.

But if you are going this far, why depend on rumor at all? When American Telephone and Telegraph Co. set out to eliminate 24,000 jobs over the next fifteen months, Robert E. Allen, chairman and chief executive officer announced the proposal immediately to all employees. No one, including the union, was happy, but at least people had time to plan for their future, although of course no one knew yet what future to plan for. And the company had something to gain by this announcement: to the extent that employees left voluntarily, the termination costs, estimated at $900 million, would be reduced. Unfortunately, such openness does not dispel rumor entirely; the problem persists.

In the long run, with one exception, disclosure problems will dissipate like morning clouds when the reorganization does, in the end, become known and take place. The exception is the premature, voluntary exit of valuable employees. Sensing unknown perils, some of them may pick up and find jobs elsewhere. The more easily they can do so, the more company-damaging, in all probability, is their loss.

The Planner should enunciate, then, a policy on disclosures: full announcement, total secrecy, or attempted confidentiality. To allay the misgivings of key employees, the policy may include a confidential advance approach to them to assure them of continued company status.

COMPANY CLIMATE

Some thought should be given to the postreorganization company climate. Is there a preference for maintaining its present state or for trying to work into something different? Is it to lean, as one expert put it, toward that of the Marine Corps or that of a sorority house?

The decision has some bearing on the kind of persons to be selected for managerial posts. Here is a natural top-sergeant whose division cooperates with no others and yet he has managed to work up to a general's slot—that is, a vice presidency. And here is a seemingly wishy-washy vacillator who nevertheless accommodates everyone quickly and well. And here is a backslapping alcoholic who in his sober moments runs the most productive sales region. And here is one of nature's noblemen, whose employees will make any sacrifice; yet he is always at odds with that top-sergeant, to the company's detriment. Which one will best fit the organization being designed:

do you want a company population that is, as geneticists would say, homozygous or heterozygous?

Anyone designing a company should certainly evolve a policy as to what kind of company it is to be, and what kind of people are to typify its ranks.

CENTRALITY

To centralize or decentralize the company's facilities, management, or staff services, should probably be covered in the objectives statement. If it is not, a policy should be adopted, reinforced with supporting reasons, to the effect that the structure aimed for is to be either centralized or decentralized.

ORIENTATION

Another guideline, if not already stated in the mission of the Planner, is whether a functional or a product orientation is sought. Total consistency is not essential. For example, orientation of the company as a whole: functional; of its marketing department: product. Orientation of the large eastern division: product; of the smaller western one: functional.

DIRECT VS. INDIRECT

How to handle the question of direct vs. indirect supervision is an organization policy that must be clearly understood.

Direct supervision: boss hires, fires, promotes, or demotes employee and tells employee what to do. Indirect supervision: staff supervisor tells another boss's employee how to do work. For example, production department clerks in one of a string of factories are directly supervised by foremen or forewomen of departments in which they work. But they record time and production in ways dictated by the factory controller, who is thus their indirect supervisor. The factory controller in turn reports directly to the factory manager, but operates according to systems and procedures emanating from the headquarters controller covering all factories. The headquarters controller is an indirect supervisor of factory accounting.

In companies with branches conflict easily erupts between solid-line authority and dotted-line accountability. Thus, the central office facilities manager may say, "No way am I going to be accountable for the safety and performance of factory facilities unless factory engineers report directly to me!" Says the central controller, "How can I guarantee the accuracy of the factory books unless I have hire-and-fire power over factory accountants?" Central Industrial Relations: "Put the local industrial relations manager under the factory manager and they'll give the place away just to keep everybody happy." (Factory manager: "Huh! You already gave it away last contract time.") And so on with Purchasing, Traffic, Data Processing, Scheduling, Medical, and in fact any central group represented in the field. Not all this is mere empire building; and it does not swell the total payroll; and it does spring from a genuine desire to control one's responsibilities in the best possible way. But carried to its extreme it leaves the factory manager, for example, with little but a corps of forepersons and time for long afternoons at the local club. Ten central departments are managing his factory for him.

To give the Planner firm ground to stand on, there should be a company policy on the uses of direct (solid-line) and indirect (dotted-line) authority.

CHECKS AND BALANCES

Preservation of a system of checks and balances is essential for the company's protection. But it is easily violated in the enthusiasm of combining what seem to be natural allies. "Let's see, why not blend Accounts Payable into Purchasing? Save double handling, paperwork, computer time, and supervision." No. "Hey, if you put Payroll Accounting and Personnel together, one tape serves two purposes." No, again. Good auditing practices say no as a matter of policy, a policy that the Planner must be aware of.

UNTOUCHABILITY

Without actually being put into writing, there may be a policy that the hand of reorganization may not touch certain pieces on the game board; for example, old Dr. Fuddy with his little, now useless, research lab. Dispensable he may be, but who developed the new adhesive thirty years ago that put the company in the big money? He did. Leave him alone.

And good, loyal Mrs. Shrude, once secretary to the vice president of sales, possessed undoubtedly of records of dinner meetings in remote places between her boss and a competitor's vice president. Now she is a supernumerary "file coordinator." Don't touch her.

And then there is the protected status that union stewards or committee persons may have been granted in the contract. It is not worth violating, especially at a time when you want cooperation from all quarters.

Some facilities, too, may be exempt. For example, the freestanding, "executive building," erected a few years ago to bring all the executive offices together so that their occupants could "interrelate," as the consultant put it. Now it might seem more sensible, and economical too, to get them back in their own divisions where they would be in closer touch with their employees. But that building cost a visible fortune and received a well-publicized decorator's award. It was in the *Fortune* writeup! Abandoning it would make the company look silly, especially to its wise-guy employees, who call it the "country club." Let it be. At least for now.

Some things are just too sacrosanct to suffer the crude molestations of reorganization.

CONSULTANTS

Not infrequently organizational improvement is suggested by management consultants as a means of saving money or revving up the company. Moreover, many consultants are expert in spotting and unraveling organizational glitches. It should be a matter of policy whether or not the Planner is to benefit from consultants' input.

CUSTOMER SERVICE

Some reorganizations spawn better customer service. Others deliberately reduce it just a little—perhaps because for certain customers at least it is costing more than it brings in. ("How much difference does it make if we don't have six people taking telephone calls on complaints?" "Do we really get anything from having salesmen make weekly visits to small-scale customers?")

It should be a policy that no reorganization that affects customer service will be approved without supporting arguments.

OUTSIDE SERVICES

Some companies prefer to do everything possible in-house. Their advertising, their medical examinations, their printing, all are done by employees. For this practice they have various reasons—economy, confidentiality, total control, habit.

Others go outside for some services to an extent that we will discuss in Chapter 7. As mentioned before, encouraging an emigration of inside work can be one of the reasons for reorganizing. It thus becomes a basis for reorganization policy: Is there any fixed commitment to staying in or going out? And if there is, does it apply to some areas but not to others—those, for example, prohibited by union agreements (painters or guards, for example)?

The Planner needs to know with how much freedom reorganization and condensation can be pursued.

NOMENCLATURE

Naming was one of Adam's first occupations. His descendants are still busy at it. Right along with the invention of the wheel went the invention of a name for that object. But sometimes naming gets to be a problem, especially in large commercial and industrial organizations.

What one conglomerate calls a "company" another calls a "division." What one company calls a "division" another calls a "department." Once you get below the department level, consistency goes still more amok: organization units are variously designated as sections, bureaus, offices, groups, or shops; and the meanings vary from company to company.

It is the same way with supervisory titles. You start out with the chairman, clear enough. Then come titles such as chief executive officer, and chief operating officer, which may coincide with either the chairman or the president or come in-between. After that there is a grab bag of supervisory titles that have significance only within the company where they are used. For example, head (as in division head or head librarian), manager, supervisor, foreman or forewoman, director (some companies restrict its use to members of the board, others have, for example, a "director of research," with no ambiguity at all), group or section leader, and chief. Sometimes these are preceded by a qualifying adjective as in *vice* president, *general* manager, *senior* department head, *assistant* or *associate* manager, or (in England) *deputy managing* director. When you get into hospitals, schools, the military, or religious bodies, additional titles are found that are peculiar to the organization: a "warden" in the Episcopal Church is not the same as a "warden" in the county jail.

Titles cause problems. One problem is that you can run out of them. Working your way down the organization chart you have, say, president, vice president, general manager, manager, department head, supervisor—now what do you call the next two levels? It is all very well to say that there should not be more than six or seven levels in the organization, but in companies with branch operations scattered around the country skyscraperism is often hard to avoid.

A second problem with titles is determining, within a company, just what they mean. Does "general manager" denote only one who is over managers? Or does it apply to anyone at a certain organizational level, regardless of what lies below—for example, might you

have a "general manager, government relations" with no subordinates at all?

A third problem with titles is a tendency to read caste or rank into
them where none really exists. "My position should be called 'general
manager' " says the manager for public relations. "But you don't have
any managers reporting to you." "Yes, but a lot of my work is dealing
with general managers and it would materially assist me to have the
same title they do." Sometimes employees think title governs salary
level (sometimes it really does, though it should not), and think the
best source of a raise is a title change.

People hunger for titles. Just try transferring someone, even with
no loss in pay, from a position designated "manager" to one called
"section head," for the sole sake of building broader experience as a
basis for future promotion, and see what the reaction is. Perhaps titles
should be deliberately employed as a device motivating employees
for advancement. But desire for prestige does not necessarily accompany capability for performance. In fact, just as an offer of free cocaine
would motivate some people to seek advancement, but in a way irrelevant to company goals, so does title-dangling motivate exactly
those employees least qualified, both emotionally and intellectually,
for positions of responsibility, and for the wrong reasons. Conversely,
explicitly lower-level titles confirm a feeling of limited responsibility.
"Don't ask me: I'm only a department head." Not only that, title
distinctions erect false psychological barriers between people. They
encourage status confrontation and pseudo-authority in dealings as
opposed to simple reliance on facts.

Few companies would suffer from an absence of title distinctions.
Nomenclature should certainly be considered among the policies governing reorganization. Suppose that as a matter of policy the title
"manager" were assigned wholesale to any responsible position below the level of vice president, from "manager, labor relations" all
the way down to "manager, mail room," with managers reporting to
managers? It is an easy out, costs nothing, and palliates Type A
behavior.

PERSONNEL MATTERS

Any reorganization comes as a blessing to some employees, a ca-
tastrophe to others. Some are happy because they were promoted,
transferred to more congenial work, or even allowed to flourish in their
niches in a smoother-running business. Others are unhappy because
they were demoted, unfavorably transferred, or let go. Reorganization
colors employees' welfare, and because their welfare is the lifeblood
of morale, it colors the company's too.

Even after it is over and done with, a residual gnawing resentment may linger, to say nothing of a fear of what will happen if a firestorm sweeps over the company again. So how employees will be dealt with influences the success of the project and should be known to the Planner.

Monetary elements bulk big in the employee algorithm. For example:

- Severance Pay—Does the company have a severance pay formula in place or will it have to set one up—say a week's pay for every year of service, plus accumulated vacation pay? Will it provide extended insurance? Will payment be contingent on the employee's continuing to work through some specified date? Such a provision ensures against employees taking off too soon when they are still needed in place to assist with transition or shut-down of facilities.

- Unemployment Compensation—Will released employees be made eligible for it and what effect will this have on the company's insurance rates?

- Pension Vesting—Who is eligible and what is the cost?

- Retirement Eligibility—Will special arrangements be made to encourage early retirement? With what effect? (DuPont offered a generous early re-tirement plan to its employees and 11,200 took off, almost twice as many as expected. "Devastating," said a headquarters manager.)[1] Incidentally, if a special early retirement package is being offered in order to encourage voluntary force reduction, it is a good idea to get it out early, at least a month before the reorganization is expected to occur. This gives people time to think about it and report their decision. That way the Planner, when redoing the organization charts and making head counts, has a better fix on where there are empty spots. (Another good idea is to make sure that all those early retirements are not promptly replaced with new hires.)

- Special Arrangements—For some departing employees special arrange-ments may be made—phone answering and secretarial assistance, perhaps a temporary office on- or off-site, resumé service, outplacement counseling, continued use of the company car for a period of time, or prolonged in-surance. Released top executives may have provisions, written or unwrit-ten, dealing with stock options, salary continuation, bonuses, job search expenses, "consulting" fees, and the like.

- Demotion Pay—Some companies pay demoted employees the wage or sal-ary of the position descended to. Others maintain present salary until (if ever) bracket increases catch up to it.

- Promotion Pay—When an employee is promoted to a higher-paying position companies variously: (1) Make no salary adjustment until after a trial pe-riod; or (2) Adjust salary upward to the full minimum of the new job, regardless of the percentage increase this entails; or (3) Adjust salary up-ward in time-spread increments to that of the new job, so the employee won't get too big a raise all at once (this has the immediate unfair effect of paying the employee less than peers on the job and also less than would go to a newcomer hired off the street); or (4) Adjust salary upward to more than the minimum of the new job, if that minimum is no more than the present salary. Which of these practices will obtain under the reorganization should be understood, as they affect implementation arrangements, morale, and cost.

• Emotional Problems—Not to be overlooked is the emotional impact on those who must make the change come to pass. Supervisors from the lowest to the highest often discover a great reluctance to tell an employee that a parting of the ways is nigh. With some it is pity, with some fear of being regarded as a bad guy, with some a simple dread of confrontation and emotional displays. ("How can I fire a vice president whose wife and mine belong to the same bridge club?" the president asks his pillow in the middle of the night.) In factories and unionized offices it may not be quite so bad: seniority governs, an impersonal law that everyone has to accept. Otherwise there may seem to be some personal element of judgment that no one likes to be stuck with. As one consequence they may hesitate to nominate specific employees or positions for release. The reorganization has run into a morale hangup. But if the budget permits generous and helpful exit arrangements, supervisors may feel better equipped to tackle the problem. And once safely through it, and having had a taste of blood, they will do it more willingly next time. Some people, sad to say, even come to regard firing as a personal skill.

DEPARTURE SELECTION

When quantities of employees are to be released from the company, a question arises: how are they to be selected? With the shutdown of a branch or a department, the deed answers the question. Everybody goes. But slimming down rather than total exodus presents alternatives. For example, seniority may govern (it almost certainly will if a union is present) and as a result longer-tenured employees are retained. On the other hand, culling-out regardless of seniority may be seen as an opportunity to peel off the least productive or the most troublesome employees, the ones who should have been fired anyway, except that nobody got around to it. Presumably this approach ensures the strengthening of what is left of the organization. A third possibility is a combination of the first two: first get rid of the incompetents, then if this is not enough start cutting rungs from the bottom of the seniority ladder. It may be objected that this immediately deprives the company of young blood that is sorely needed for the future, and so it will if the company has been following an illegal practice of hiring only people below a specified age. Too bad. In any case, a policy on releases should be in place before decisions have to be made on specific names.

If the policy says seniority governs, it will further have to pin down whether departmental, location, or company-wide seniority is the criterion. If, alternatively, it says merit (or lack of it) governs, it will have to cope with the question of who decides on merit. If a boss is being replaced because of incompetency, can you rely on his or her appraisals of those beneath who are to be selectively weeded out?

COST OF CHANGE

Few reorganizations are made without the hope that they will improve profits (or reduce losses). Conversely, none should be made with the expectation that they will be costless. The various personnel arrangements just reviewed do not come for free. Moreover, there may be writedowns, employee transfer expenses, and rearrangements of facilities, all of which must be taken into account.

But what will all this expense amount to? Does its effect on the company budget and cash requirements have to be calculated before approval? Is there a policy lid on affordable reorganization expense? If so, the Planner should be prepared to come up with estimates.

UNION PARTICIPATION

Repellent though it may seem to some executives, there are situations where union officials must be notified in advance of a reorganization affecting their members' tenure or pay. And even when there are not, prior notification may keep their feathers down. It will forestall a humiliating inability to respond to members' questions and may even promote a kind of fatalistic cooperation. The Planner should know if union relations are to be part of the reorganization plan.

PUBLICITY

Way down the road lies the reorganization itself. When it comes to pass, who outside the company hears of it? Will there be communication to community leaders? Press releases? We will have more to review about this in Chapter 11. But it is well to know in advance whether the company wants to be characteristically closed-mouth or characteristically open, so that planning can include any special arrangements necessary.

BACKUP

One policy that can hang heavy over any reorganization plan is the company's policy on backups. ("You've left out the assistant treasurer." "Well, there isn't really so much to be done at that level that you need what amounts to two executives." "Yeah, but what if the treasurer gets killed by a golf ball? Who handles the job? It's our policy to have a standby for every position.") Some companies prefer double coverage. It is a form of insurance against interruption. Others cannot support the cost. ("*Two* microbiologists in the waste-treatment lab, just in case? Do you have two furnaces in your house? Let's take our chances with one.")

Maybe the company has a genuine, thought-out policy on backup and standby and maybe it does not. Sometimes you will find a policy in one division and an opposite in another. It is a good thing to get straightened out for reorganization planning.

MINORITIES

A guideline so obvious that it may not even have to be stated is the need to be conscious of minority rights and opportunities. Something is awfully wrong with a plan that comes up with involuntary terminations heavily loaded with employees over fifty years old. Something is right with one that finds upward-bound spots for competent nonwhites and women. Reorganization is a good time for a company to get good law and good policy into action.

CONCLUSION

With reorganization objectives and guidelines/policies in place the planning process is ready to begin. The Planner is going to be creating proposed new organization charts. Compared to the old ones they will display repositioned blocks and names. New departments and positions will materialize, while some of the previous ones will drop out of sight. But while this alteration may be done behind doors in a closed room, it canot be done in a closed room of knowledge. It requires thorough insight into the purposes and functions of every element of the organization being remodeled. Let us look at some of the background information that should be available.

NOTE

1. *Wall Street Journal*, 9 April 1985.

4

Background Information

Among famous opening lines there is of course that first sentence in *Anna Karenina*: "Happy families are all alike; every unhappy family is unhappy in its own way." But the next sentences are worth noticing too: "Everything was in confusion in the Oblonsky's house.... Every person in the house felt that the stray people brought together by chance in any inn had more in common with one another than they." Why, the Oblonskys sound just like many a modern company.

Employees of happy companies unite in focusing on their product, customers, finances, and probably their competitors. Those of unhappy ones run in all directions. Some are obsessed with trying to please investors, financial analysts, and bankers. Others are preoccupied with internal rights, prerogatives, status, systems, and whatever gimmickry of scientific management is this year's rage. Falling market share, torpid sales volume, and sagging profits are peripheral issues. These employees are confused without knowing it; they are the Oblonsky family grown large.

Planners find themselves dealing with both happy and unhappy organizations. The happy ones are reorganizing in order to be prepared for an even happier future; the unhappy ones, in order to dispel that confusion that diverts their activities from the product/customer/consumer goals that should preoccupy them. What the Planner must do is get acquainted with the situation that calls for change.

It might seem as if those initiating a move would have a good grasp of what is to be done. So they may, in a general sense. But it may not be an all-encompassing grasp. The president detonating a major reorganization may know what is to be done with large divisions and with principal executives. But no president is apt to be fully informed on the many departments and positions all down the line.

At the other end of the scale, a lower-level manager contemplating a reorganization of only one or two departments may fully understand that limited domain, without taking into consideration the effect on other departments not directly involved. The Initiators of a project must depend on the Planner to fashion all its components. Ergo, the Planner must learn about those components.

As part of the planning process background information must be obtained. It may flow from:

- The strategic business plan
- The company and departmental budgets
- Personal interviews
- Standard procedure instructions
- Job descriptions
- Department descriptions
- Personal performance appraisals
- Eligibility charts
- Organization charts.

What may be expected from these follows.

STRATEGIC BUSINESS PLAN

These days strategic business planning is in the driver's seat of almost any company. Large firms employ it because their competitors do. Small ones because their bankers expect it of them. Consultants sell it. Professors teach it. It has both its own mystique and its own technique, and a jargon to go along.

Nested within a really professional five-year plan are one-year plans, and within them there may be found sales plans, product and market development plans, media plans, promotional plans, research plans, human resource plans, facilities plans, and an assortment of financial plans. By rights there should be an organizational evolution plan too. None of this is just squirreled away in people's heads. It is mounted in text, charts, and tables, reinforced with slides or film strips for presentation, and perhaps also stowed away in the computer's discs, tapes, and chips. It can be accessed.

Not all formal business plans command the same degree of adherence. In some companies the planning process itself is what firms up a consensus on direction to be taken. Once constructed, the plan is filed away until next year's update. In others the plan is the very course by which the plane flies, and frequent trackings and corrective actions are built into it like an autopilot.

Certainly any reorganization should be consonant with the aims of the business plan. What is ahead should guide what is done today. For example, if there is desire for a line of "cash-cow" products, well-milked, to be sold off next year to another company, it might make sense to begin now to isolate their marketing, sales, and facilities, along with the associated personnel. If the plan visualizes rapid growth of a new product, today's reorganization may establish the nucleus of that product's future organizational placement. If the plan prescribes a gradual transition from family to professional management, the reorganization may anticipatorily tighten up areas of authority now.

Though the pages of charts, tables, and forecasts that swell many business plans may not be of great use to the reorganization Planner, the overall objectives, goals, and descriptive statements that usually preface a business plan provide invaluable guidance.

But though it is invaluable, this guidance is still provisional. A five-year business plan has a way of changing long before the fifth year. For example, the plan:

- Is simply too optimistic. And why not? A plan that predicts no improvement will only stimulate demands for one that overcomes a pessimistic future.
- Is based on the same surveys and demographics that competitors use. If everyone counts on picking from the same tree, someone is going to have to climb back down to find another. A change of plan becomes necessary.
- Relies too introspectively on the success of the company's own strategies without foreseeing competitors'. It is like trying to plan the outcome of a game of draw poker.
- Does not allow for the unexpected: supply failures, economic recessions, capital unavailability, lawsuits, disasters, changing consumer tastes (who would have expected video games, with a new market of kids coming along every year, to wilt so quickly?).
- Falls victim to a new CEO, who has ideas altogether different from his predecessor's (the board devoutly hopes).

The Planner should be fully congnizant of the business plan's requirements for an organization to support it. At the same time the Planner must follow the strategic plan's progress from year to year to detect organization-affecting revisions.

BUDGET

Where there is a company there is a budget. Business plans (written or not) and budgets abound. There may be businesses that run without them, but they are seldom of much size, rarely public, and certainly not dependent on assistance from lending institutions, who expect to find these organs as a neurosurgeon expects to find a brain in his patient's skull.

Occasionally, to the disinterested observer, they may seem to be overemphasized. Is it possible that their construction and repeated revision before approval, together with the hours of tracking, follow-up, explaining, excusing, and justifying that they entail occupy as much as 10 percent of the upper-level year—time that might more rewardingly have been spent on dealing with products, customers, and consumers? Yes, it is. But what is the alternative? Some day, no doubt, one will be found, along with the common cold cure. In the meantime we struggle as best we can with these time-usurping necessities of good management.

Even more than the business plan, the company budget comprises many parts: subsidiaries' budgets, divisional budgets, departmental budgets, capital budgets, expense budgets, and more. Many of these are of interest to the Planner. For one thing, they show where the money is flowing; possible sinkholes of expense to be probed. They answer questions: What is the collective cost of supervision at each level—for example, of all vice presidents, all division heads, all general managers, all department heads? What as a matter of fact, is the overall cost of supervision per employee? For how many "live" dollars are individual positions accountable? What savings may be attributed to the elimination of individual positions? What additional expenses are additional positions likely to incur? What occupancy expense can be saved through combination of locations? What additional positions are budgeted and what happens to them in reorganization?

Many expense factors can be obtained most accurately by resort to those persons directly involved. But for a first estimate, and a confidential one, the budget is a useful reference.

PERSONAL INTERVIEWS

A great source of background information is personal interviews. After all, the Planner is dealing with an organization, and an organization is people, so why not talk to people about the organization they serve in? Provided the mere thought of reorganizing is not going to produce mass nervous collapse, it is a good idea.

Now of course if the main point of the change is to prune 10 percent of the names from the payroll, there is not much point in extended palaver. About all you can do is tell a supervisor, "By ten o'clock tomorrow give me the names of six people to be let go from your department. Keep EEO in mind and don't discuss this with anyone else." Well, maybe that is a little bald, but you get the idea.

On the other hand, a reorganization genuinely intended to improve the company's performance can only benefit from an internal survey.

Not everything about an organization is known to those in its upper levels. They are sort of in Plato's cave, looking at the shadows on the walls (though not, I must add, of the "ideal"). They often do not know each employee, they may not understand the importance of arcane technology, they may not even know what some departments do ("I hate to say it," says the vice president, engineering and construction, "but I've always wondered what goes on in that 'fulfillment department' over in Marketing. Do you suppose...?") In their excusable ignorance they are not in a good position to devise, let alone evaluate, every possible improvement. The Planner has probably been selected as a person who is fairly well-informed. But even the Planner may find unfamiliar thickets in the forest.

Most of what I have been saying applies to larger companies. But small ones, too, harbor areas for exploration. With the presidents' preoccupation with markets, customers, legal matters, and finance, opportunities for attending to internal problems may get neglected. They know that talking to employees about how to reorganize the company for greater effectiveness is a good idea, but where is the time for it?

Given the benefits of interviewing, who should do it? Perhaps the Planner is not prepared or available for the task. In fact, the job may be done more productively by a third party drawn from the outside, someone skilled in interviewing itself. A good source of such talent is the "soft-science" faculty of a college or university: perhaps a professor of psychology or sociology, for example; one who is fairly level-headed, confidence-generating, reasonably folksy, and not too doctrinaire.

After being appointed, the interviewer is introduced to the executive group. The intention to obtain objective information is explained as well as the interviewer's ability to use good judgment and preserve confidentiality. The executive group is asked to pass this information down to lower strata, request cooperation, and facilitate the interviewer's progress with introductions as necessary. (Or a general explanatory letter may be sent to employees.)

"Hi," the professor says, dropping into someone's chair after being introduced. "I'm just going around collecting good ideas. What do you and this department do? And what would you change if you could? I've got a terrible memory, so d'you mind if I take notes? It's all confidential as to source." Then the interviewer smiles and sits back.

Who should be interviewed? It seems fairly obvious that all executives, managers, and supervisors in areas apt to be affected ought to be talked to. So should organizational neighbors involved in transactions with their areas. A sales department reorganization might, for example, profit from the input of marketing people. The factory managers might have some thoughts about intended improvements in Engineering's organization. People from Auditing and Systems are often closely aware of the strengths and flaws of organizational networks. Nor should hourly employees who, like the stockroom clerk or the head mechanic, occupy de facto liaison positions, be overlooked.

Of course the process cannot cover everyone. It can be only a sample. But the sample should be carefully thought out in advance. If out of seven departmental forepersons, the interviewer talks to six and skips the seventh, that seventh is going to be tizzy-struck.

Out of such interviews naturally flows a recognizable stream of self-serving, excusing, blaming, and territorial ambition. At the same time good insights and suggestions also appear, on such widely disparate subjects as

- the existence of dead-end jobs
- uncertainties as to full vs. shared accountabilities
- nonexistence of accountabilities that should be in place
- untapped talents
- duplicate, overlapping, unnecessary, or conflicting functions
- ill-coordinated functions
- indirect lines of supervision
- emulation figures
- internal hostilities and rivalries
- unofficial, informal, and advantageous cooperation
- overloaded or underloaded positions
- understaffed, undersupported, or underequipped activities
- unintegrated functions
- physical space and equipment problems
- misplaced functions
- security vulnerabilities.

Most of these topics deal with organization rather than personality issues; it is not an attitude survey that is being conducted. An interviewer's sense, however, of generally felt problems, is not to be despised. The manager who looks brilliant from the top but a very dull gray when seen from below, is a bird well worth spotting. So is that manager targeted by an executive for expulsion who is paradoxically viewed with respect by peers and subordinates. Such a manager should perhaps be more appropriately assigned.

The interviewer, who has been given a deadline, summarizes findings and recommendations in a written report. Ordinarily it is not too great an idea to publicize these results. They are meant for immediate application, not speculation. An oral presentation to the executive group, however, may be helpful. After all, those people are pretty much running the company and have a right to know what is going on.

An interviewer's report then joins the collection of background information.

A second set of interviews goes on between the Planner and the persons who have initiated the proposed reorganization in the first place. Its purpose is to express those specific changes that the Initiators have visualized as accomplishing the objectives already spelled out. It may cover two fields: people and structure.

With regard to people, the Initiators may have individuals in mind for certain key spots. "I want to move Hanks from vice president of sales to a new position, vice president of strategic planning," says the CEO; "and I want to move Banks up to the sales slot." "Two of the product managers, Burke and Hare, ought to be interchanged in their positions to deepen their experience." "Box doesn't know it, but he's going to elect early retirement, and we're putting Cox in his job. But who's in line for Cox's job? I'm not certain."

As to structure, the Initiators undoubtedly entertain some definite architectural details that will give shape to the overall objectives. They will talk these over with the Planner, sketching alternative organization charts until a workable prototype emerges. "This is pretty much what I had in mind," says the CEO looking at a rough organization chart that he has drawn; "but how those labs are to be split out is too much for me. Maybe you'd better talk to the vice president of research about that."

These interviews on people and structure for the new organization are part background information and part preliminary planning.

STANDARD PROCEDURE INSTRUCTIONS

On the bookshelves of many large companies, and of some of the more orderly small ones too, are volumes of what are known as "Standard Procedure Instructions" (SPIs). For stupefying reading these cannot be beat. Who initiates, who approves, who receives copies of this, that, or the other piece of paperwork (or data process) that is emblematic representation of an activity: a purchase, a sale, a hire, a performance of a service—any transaction among entities in the large group—is their pallid life blood. From one point of view, SPIs are the very cloak of bureaucracy; from another, the distilled essence of system, uniformity, and control. If their fault is life-curdling dullness, their virtue is reduction of business disorder to simple, reliable routine. Executives seldom have need to resort to them. But for the perplexed employee their help echoes the sixteenth century promise: "Everyman, I will go with thee, and be thy guide, in thy most need to stand by thy side."

SPIs are not always available in the form of these books I mention. They may be absorbed into the systems tucked away in data processing departments where they function automatically. In any case they reflect the coursing of information in the company—a flow that may be responsible in itself for organization proliferation.

No Planner, however conscientious, should undertake to study through a company's SPIs all at once. They tend to induce a creeping somnolence. Still, they should not be ignored, for embedded in them, like buckshot in a carcass, are clues to how the organization has come to be what it is. A labyrinthine procedure for accomplishing a simple purpose; a blizzard of approvals that signify only passage over a desk; a multitude of file copies that clog someone's time and somebody's file space—here is symptomatic evidence of a spreading disease that bloats the organization. On the good side, the SPIs tell how departments connect with one another. They designate who does what, how it is done, and often why. They record interrelationships that might be condensed or combined for savings in positions and in action time. They sometimes neatly clothe policy in a way that relieves employees of divers decisions, making their jobs easier and, more to the point, lower-payable.

But they cannot always undergird reorganization. When a new CEO has replaced a faltering predecessor, and has fired four incompatible vice presidents, and brought in three loyal ones who are impatient to reshape the organization in the image of ones they have just left, there just is not time for the Planner to explore details. Why bother? Speed and sudden change are everything and shattering old procedures is a way of destroying frozen bureaucracy.

Nevertheless, for insight into the organization, SPIs are worth a read. Even a new executive, company-ignorant, may poke around in them to get a view of what goes on.

JOB DESCRIPTIONS AND EVALUATIONS

Anyone remodeling an organization is bound to be familiar with many of its jobs. But lurking in the crevices are positions that are unfamiliar. Here in the merchandising department is something called "coordinator." Coordinator of what? Is this position performing an essential function? Why is that function essential to begin with? Is it instead a make-work position for an employee past his or her prime? Or could "coordinator" be the misnomer given to a female who took over her boss's job (but not his salary) when he was promoted?

Job descriptions, if they are available, help to educate the Planner on the content of positions. This content is not always apparent in the position title. Some positions have grandiose titles—the author once knew a laborer in a steel pipe mill who had his title, Pipe Disburser, printed on calling cards to impress casual acquaintances in bars—and others, like that coordinator, are impenetrable. You have to read the job description.

It would be nice if all job descriptions told a simple, clear story. But not all companies have good ones. Some are sketchy. Some are out of date. Some are overblown. In one company they are written by a job analyst and in another by the supervisors or incumbents, with a wide range of accuracy. But in most cases they are informative—and in two ways.

First, they tell what the particular position is doing, which helps to answer doubts as to its necessity or expendability.

Second, they tell (or should tell) how the position relates to others, what strands it joins in the organizational network.

Additionally, they are thought-provoking. Say that throughout the organization are scattered a number of jobs performing similar or related functions. Would there be any advantage to bringing them together? Or are they more effective and responsive to local needs when apart, in a small-scale decentralization? Do any of them duplicate what others also do? If they use equipment, would consolidation of these functions permit less and possibly better equipment to be used?

Or say that there is a descending terrace of twelve levels of supervision before the first nonexempt or hourly employee is reached. What do all these intermediaries *do*?

Or say that a seemingly straightforward title, "manager, testing," surprisingly turns out from its job description to require not only managerial ability but postdoctoral work in nonferrous metallurgy and a knowledge of the company's secret technology. This is not a job to tinker with.

Learning from job descriptions educates the Planner, suggests opportunities, and protects against erroneous conclusions.

Closely allied to, in fact usually dependent on job descriptions, are job evaluations. Like the descriptions, they vary in reliability. Some are well-controlled. They are periodically reviewed en masse to ensure continuing internal consistency. If there has been a turnover in evaluators, careful training has preserved a uniform approach. The evaluations are as objective as possible, regardless of the incumbent of the job being examined.

One the other hand, some job evaluation systems have undergone slow sea changes over the years. Changes in duties (especially downward ones) have not been caught up in reevaluation, and pressures to make the evaluation fit the person rather than the job have not gone unheeded. There is more to them than meets the innocent eye.

In any case, good or bad, the job evaluations are what the company is living with and determining its pay scales from. Their findings are part of the company's own adjustment to its own realities. They should be available to the Planner as an index to the relative status of positions. Inadvertently putting a low-point chicken job up in a high-point eagle's aerie or dealing too freely with an "assistant-to" who has surprisingly high points because he or she is in effect actually running a division while the boss is on the road—these are misplays that reference to recorded point evaluations can prevent.

DEPARTMENT DESCRIPTIONS

Though job descriptions tell what everybody does in an organization, they really do not tell what the organization itself does, any more than separate snapshots of a carburetor's parts convey a sense of an assembled and functioning carburetor. For a better grasp of what is going on department descriptions deserve attention.

Unlike job descriptions, department descriptions are not a staple of the literature on personnel management. Job descriptions are an essential adjunct to wage and salary evaluation. They are in wide use, and their format has become more or less standardized, with some tailoring to fit the particular evaluation system in effect. Department descriptions, on the other hand, have no technical tie-in at all. Their end purpose is only to describe. Costing time and money to prepare, they may easily be neglected. And yet that end purpose—mere description—can be put to good use.

Figure 4.1 shows an example of a department description in skeleton format.

To those reading it, the department description can

- Explain the department's purpose and reason for being.
- Describe what the department does (and does not) do.
- Clarify for what things the department (1) has first and final responsibility, and (2) has shared responsibility with other departments, necessitating cooperation.

```
┌──────────────────────────────────────────────────────────────┐
│                   DEPARTMENT DESCRIPTION                        │
├──────────────────────────────────────────────────────────────┤
│  Department Name  _____         Date_____            │
│                                                                 │
│  Division Name       _____   Location_____            │
└──────────────────────────────────────────────────────────────┘
```

1.   PRIMARY MISSION (descriptive paragraph)

2.   ORGANIZATION

    a.   Number of budgeted employees: _____

    b.   Structure: (Attach organization chart of

        (i)   department, and
        (ii) department or division of which it is part)

3.   DOLLARS CONTROLLED

    a.   Department budget: $ _____

    b.   Book value of assets controlled: $ _____

4.   INTERNAL CONTACTS

    (Describe nature of contacts with other departments)

5.   EXTERNAL CONTACTS

    (Describe nature of contacts with outsiders such as suppliers,
      professionals, customers, associations, and government bodies)

6.   PRIMARY RESPONSIBILITIES (itemize)

7.   SHARED RESPONSIBILITIES   (itemize)

Figure 4.1

- Define areas in which departments have differentiation of function: those in which they have initiatory, as opposed to supporting roles; and specialization of skills as opposed to general reliance on skills of others.
- Define areas in which departments have integration of function: those in which various departments must be interdependent, cooperative, and intercommunicative.
- Disclose any overlaps or gaps between various departments.
- Give all members of a department knowledge of its role, and a sense of common purpose transcending individual job boundaries.
- Assist in performing periodic audits.

One more thing department descriptions offer is the opportunity to move toward a more open, contributory style of working. Job descriptions isolate positions, and the employees who fill them, into separate cells. Each cell has its prescribed list of duties and responsibilities. People do not move freely, in the course of the workday, from one cell to another. They are concerned with meeting the job's— the cell's—requirements. They tend to protect their cells. They experience a sense of apartness. They don't meddle in other people's jobs. Their scale of intensity is first, the position; second, the department; third, the company. Would it not be more productive, some observers of management have thought, if the cell walls were dissolved?

At the very least this approach would identify employees not as the occupants of rigidly defined positions but as members of a freely interactive group. Released from their job position cells, all the employees of a department are at liberty to work jointly for the department's perfection.

In such an environment department descriptions are paramount and position descriptions may wither away. Along with them may go, with some savings in administrative expense, the job evaluations that rely on position descriptions. These may be replaced by a freer pay system based on such personal qualifications as tenure, experience, education, expertise, and job-market competitiveness. This is, in fact, exactly the situation that prevails in many small companies. Often their loose, participative internal structure is one of their greatest assets. Why should not a department be treated as if it were a small company? Having department descriptions supports the employees' belongingness.

And, just incidentally, department descriptions are of value as training aids for new employees. Even for the executive, particularly one new to the company, they provide insight into what is going on in the blocks of the new and unfamiliar organization chart that dangle like a card-shop mobile from his own cartouche.

PERSONAL PERFORMANCE APPRAISALS

Though dealing with what may seem to be merely blocks on a chart and their connecting arteries, the Planner nevertheless encounters decisions on the placement or omission of individual employees. Even though such decisions are ultimately made by line management, the Planner should be aware of their significance. To this end access to personnel records should be at least in the penumbra of background information. Of these records two relate particularly to a reorganization: personal performance appraisals and eligibility charts.

Rare is the reorganization that does not generate some promotions, demotions, and lateral transfers. Sometimes these are designed to place the best-suited person in a job; sometimes, conversely, to find the job best suited to an employee's career development; and sometimes, realistically, to remove the unqualified person.

Personal performance appraisals are intended to (1) assess how well an employee meets the goals and accountabilities of the job filled; (2) inform the employee of opportunities to improve performance; and (3) estimate the employee's readiness for future advancement. Usually they are sponsored by the personnel department. They are recorded on a form for future reference as to progress. They are conducted periodically by the employee's immediate superior, with review by the next higher level. They are semicredible.

If there is a fault with such appraisals, it lies in the personalities of the supervisors administering them. Some bosses cannot bear to tell an employee, face-to-face, of deficiencies. They are afraid of tears or argument, both demotivating. They even hate to acknowledge good performance lest it lead to an expectation of a raise. They try to gloss everything over and get it out of the way as painlessly as possible. Others, braver, speak candidly with employees and make of the appraisal process an element in the company's improvement. As for the employees, most want to know how they are doing and appreciate periodic discussion of their job performance.

In any case personal performance appraisals, viewed with a keen eye for appraiser's bias, are a handy reference for the Planner, whether people are being selected for openings or for release. While no decision should be made without direction from the relevant managerial level, the records may help to shape the outcome. This is particularly true when a new executive, rooting for change but still unfamiliar with all the people affected, is in need of guidance beyond his or her first impressions.

ELIGIBILITY CHART

An organization chart is all very fine to show where people are now, but in a reorganization it is not enough. You also need to know where people are headed. Who is ready to move up? Who is going to have to be replaced? Such questions are answered, at least in a preliminary way, by an "eligibility chart" (see Figure 4.2). An eligibility chart shows (1) who is available to fill a position should it become vacated, and (2) what the promotional opportunities are for individuals.

On such a chart, for each major position the incumbent's status is coded as either:

1. Qualified and available for promotion, or
2. Qualified for promotion, but no replacement, or

Figure 4.2

ELIGIBILITY CHART

Date: _____ Dept./Div.: _____ Prepared by: _____

Present Incumbents							Replacement Candidates					
Position	Name	0	1	2	3	4	Position	Name	1	2	3	Comment
V.P. Mktg./Sls.	T. Williams	X				X	G.M. Cons. Sls.	S. Jones	X			Retires Oct. 1
							G.M. Ind. Sls.	F. Miller	X			
							G.M. Mkts.	W. Wilson			X	Needs field experience
V.P. Opns.	E. Anderson	X				X	G.M. Mfg.	H. Taylor	X			Performance Unsatisfactory
							G.M. Engr. Design	M. Walker	X			(Now in Eng. & Res.)
V.P. Finance	J. White		X				G.M. Fin. Acctg.	A. Harris	X			
							G.M. Cost Acctg.	R. Clark			X	Needs more breadth
							G.M. Sls. Acctg.	T. Jackson		X		Should develop replacement
V.P. Engr. & Res.	H. Lewis					X						Prefers own specialty
V.P.	O. Allen				X							
G.M. Cost Acctg.	R. Clark	X			X		Sr. Cost Acct.	P. Philips	X			
							Fin. Acct.	K. Carter		X		Feels dead-ended

Promotional Status Code:

0 = Immediate attention needed

1 = Qualified and available for promotion

2 = Qualified but no replacement

3 = Potential in 1-3 years

4 = Not presently a candidate

3. Potential for promotion 1–3 years, or
4. Not presently a candidate for promotion.

It also lists backup candidates (if any) for each such position. These in turn are coded as to whether they are supported by replacement candidates or are on the way to availability. A space for comments permits some elaboration. For example, in Figure 4.2, T. Williams is not a candidate for promotion because he is due to retire, a situation that calls for immediate attention to Williams's backup candidates. H. Lewis, the vice president of engineering and research, is quite happy in that specialized position and has no desire to move further into the quagmires of finance or operations that a president must slosh through.

If desired the chart shown in Figure 4.2 may be extended to carry even more information. We show a special "0" column to alert users to cases calling for prompt action—a pending retirement, an unsatisfactory incumbent, or an employee who is restless because dead-ended. One or two more columns might be added; for example, to indicate "lateral transfer desirable" or "replacement desirable."

Many companies use some form of the eligibility chart as a routine means of protecting organization quality. Periodically higher-level managers update it on the basis of personal knowledge and performance appraisals. With its help they can take proactive measures to anticipate changes of personnel.

For example, nothing is more disruptive than the sudden vacating of a position with no qualified person on hand to refill it. True, such situations may be created deliberately: as an opportunity to bring in new blood, for instance; or as a prelude to abolishing a position or combining it with another. But when these are not the case, the scramble to find a replacement, the uncertainties while the department runs without a head, the loss of momentum if an unprepared recruit has to be moved in, all contribute to the Oblonsky confusion of an unhappy family. The eligibility chart calls attention to such danger spots. It signals the need to prepare candidates for future advancement.

It also buttresses career path planning. It discloses the presence of individuals who, though promising, are blocked for promotion. It unveils situations where nonpromotable individuals suppress rising stars. It suggests opportunities for lateral transfer to broaden experience. It focuses attention on spots where more backup is needed to free employees to advance.

In reorganization the eligibility chart is a valuable resource. From it a tentative hint can be obtained as to which individuals do or do not belong in a strengthened company. If incumbents are expected to depart through early retirement or outright release, the feasibility of replacing them can be established. Where departments are to be combined, the choice of members can be evaluated.

Like personal performance appraisals, eligibility charts are by no means totally reliable. For one thing, they are sketchy. No decision should be based on them alone without further investigation. Worse, if the reorganization is a cutback they may, having been prepared by the company's executives and upper managers, reflect the very biases that have got the company in trouble. One man's protégé is another man's wimp. Conversely, in an expansion reorganization, they reflect the good sense that has enabled the company to grow. In any case they are an asset that the Planner cannot overlook.

ORGANIZATION CHARTS

Of all the background information needed, organization charts of the existing company structure are the most indispensable. They come in different models, and in Chapters 5 and 6 we will examine their characteristics and use.

5

Organization Charts I

With background information in place detailed planning begins. This consists of two phases (1) planning the nature of the change; and (2) planning the implementation of the change.

In planning the nature of the change, that is, what the change will consist of, it is difficult to escape using organization charts. We are going to look at various kinds of charts and at the signals they emit for organizational improvement.

ROSTER

The simplest organization chart is scarcely a chart at all, but a roster. It lists the sundry positions in an organization, with successive indentations for lower levels of hierarchy. Opposite each position is the name of the incumbent.

Figure 5.1 shows such a roster. For each of the positions on it there may be subsidiary rosters into the depths of the organization.

These charts have their advantages. Unlike more graphic ones, which require drafting or special computer software, they are easy to keep updated on word processing equipment. They are compact. They serve as an organizational index, making it easy to look up who handles a certain responsibility. They lend themselves to ready reference for other purposes as well; for example, the processor can be programmed (with suitable safeguards on confidential information) to list after each name such ancillary data as telephone number, job number, age, exempt status, appraisal rating, or promotional eligi-

ORGANIZATION ROSTER

President . . . . O. Smith

   Administrative Assistant . . . . V. Johnson

   Secretary . . . . E. Brown

   Vice President, Marketing & Sales . . . . R. Williams

      Gen. Mgr. Consumer Sales . . . . S. Jones

      Gen. Mgr. Industrial Sales . . . . F. Miller

      Gen. Mgr. Trade Relations . . . . V. Davis

      Gen. Mgr. Marketing . . . . W. Wilson

   Vice President, Operations . . . . E. Anderson

      Gen. Mgr. Manufacturing . . . . H. Taylor

      Gen. Mgr. Transportation & Warehousing . . . . . M. Moore

      Gen. Mgr. Production & Inventory . . . . M. Thomas

      Gen. Mgr. Quality Control . . . . M. Martin

      Gen. Mgr. Purchasing . . . . T. Thompson

   Vice President, Engineering & Research . . . . H. Lewis

      Gen. Mgr. Engineering Design . . . . M. Walker

      Gen. Mgr. Facilities . . . . N. Hall

      Gen. Mgr. Research . . . . L. Robinson

   Vice President, Finance . . . . J. White

      Gen. Mgr. Financial Accounting . . . . A. Harris

      Gen. Mgr. Sales Accounting . . . . T. Jackson

      Gen. Mgr. Cost Accounting . . . . R. Clark

   Vice President, Strategic Planning . . . . O. Allen

Figure 5.1

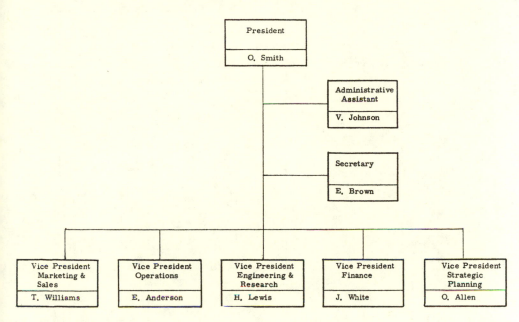

Figure 5.2

bility. But with all these advantages rosters do not lend themselves to organizational analysis and planning. They are too compressed.

SIMPLE BLOCK CHART

The more open format of block charts shows essentially the same information as a roster, but in a pictorial manner that appeals to the right as well as the left side of the brain. It gives a better sense of relationships. The interlocks that are implied in the very word "organization" stand out more clearly. Each block, or cartouche, occupies its position of superiority or subordination to other blocks. Figure 5.2 shows a typical example.

Similar charts can be made for each of the vice presidents shown on this one, a page to each. But for reorganization study it may be better to start with a more inclusive chart, the kind that is hung on a wall, too big to show here except in miniature (see Figure 5.3).

To save space, immediately subordinate positions may be shown vertically on flags as shown in Figure 5.4. Then for each of these a separate chart shows further downward subdivisions.

Though indispensable, charts do have their limitations, and they are apt to be misinterpreted by casual viewers. Some things can not be inferred from them. For example:

Figure 5.3

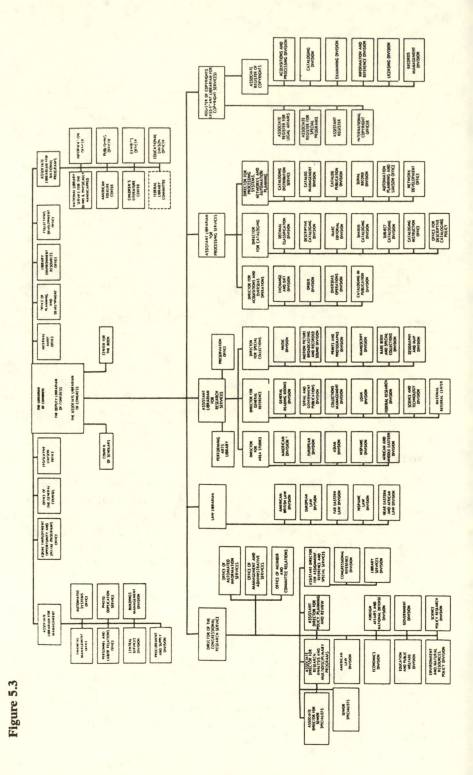

64

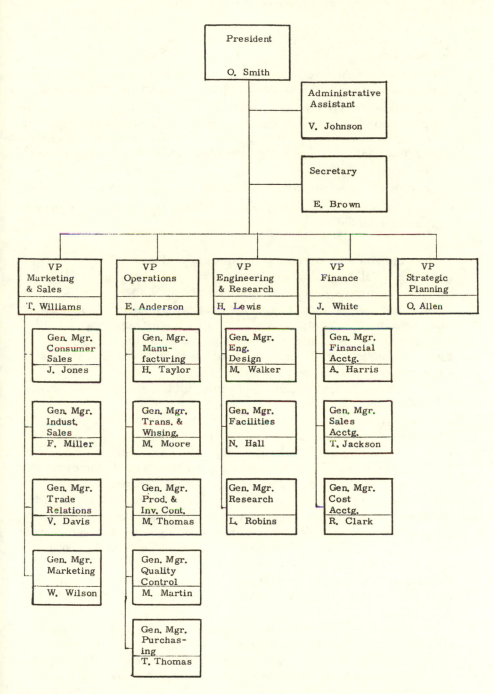

Figure 5.4

65

- The vertical lines reveal only direct, not functional, or indirect, authority or supervision.
- The levels at which boxes are shown do not correspond to salary groupings. Two boxes at the same level may carry different compensation ranges.
- The position of the boxes does not indicate "status," value to the company, incumbent-ability, or extent of accountability. A high-demand professional position, for example, may merely, because of the number of layers of supervision, fall lower on a chart than the supervisor of many low-skill employees.
- The vertical lines on the chart do not necessarily depict lines of promotion.
- The size of the boxes does not necessarily reflect the magnitude of the positions represented.

Block charts can also represent matrix organization. The one shown in Figure 5.5 illustrates a task force, probably ad hoc, matrix.

Matrix is usually described by writers on management as lending itself to the management of specific projects. However, it also exists unnoticed in many companies where indirect staff supervision guides localized staff. For example, as shown by dashed lines in Figure 5.6, the headquarters staff controller and chief engineer have indirect supervision over their factory counterparts.

In a matrix representation, this same relationship may be shown as in Figure 5.7.

All positions affected by reorganization should appear on block diagrams. All the names, even, of the incumbents, should be blocked in place. This may include both exempt and nonexempt salaried and hourly employees. There is something to be learned, for example, when one sees all the administrative assistants, secretaries, and typists in place with those whom they work for—paper (or computer file) generators all. In smaller companies the chart-everyone approach is not difficult and it is instructive. Suppose, however, that a financial services company has 4,000 office employees. You would like to fit them all on a chart but you can not. The "multitude makes frustrate the design," as the poet Dryden says.[1] In the small company a portion of the chart might look like Figure 5.8. In a large company, like Figure 5.9.

Not to be overlooked in chart makeup is the existence of temporary, part-time, or off-premises workers. For example, the house organ editor requisitions typists once a month from a temp-help supplier. The laboratories have college students working three afternoons a week on bench tests. The market research department engages a crew to conduct periodic interviews in supermarkets. In the accounts these quasi-employees may be charged to "purchased services" rather than

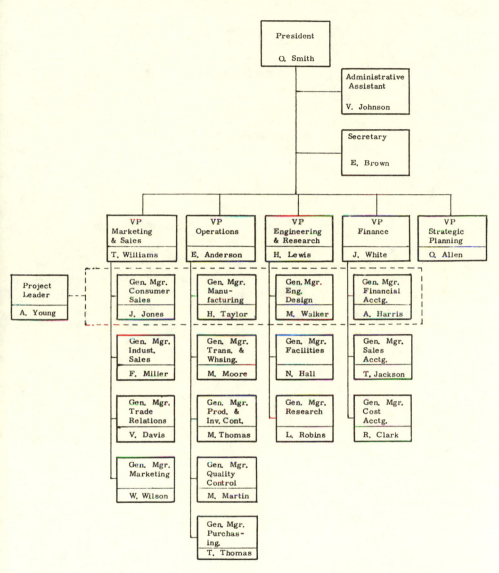

Figure 5.5

"payroll." Whatever the accounting, they should be identified on the chart by a broken rather than solid line box (see Figure 5.10).

SALARY STATUS CHART

A salary status chart is one in which the vertical placement of the blocks corresponds to wage or salary evaluated points. Positions hav-

Figure 5.6

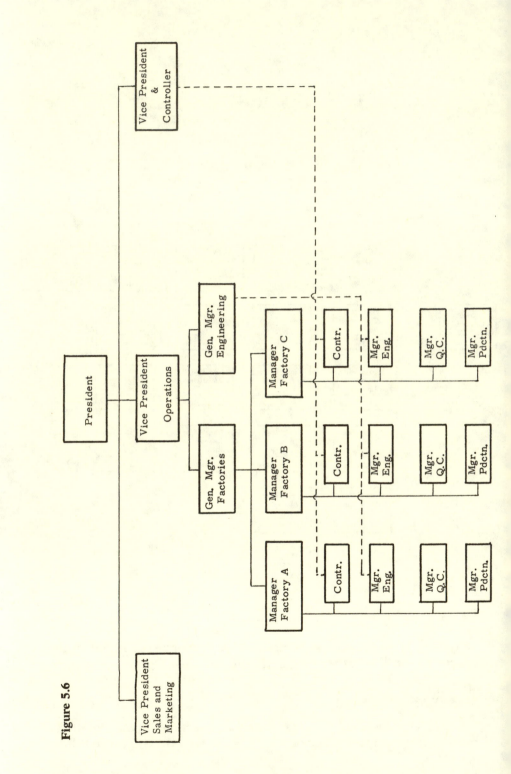

Figure 5.7

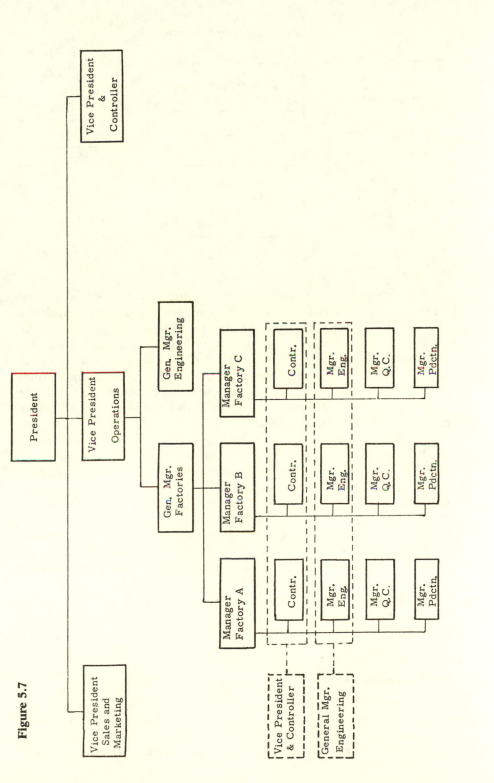

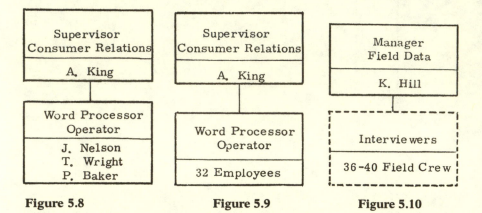

Figure 5.8   Figure 5.9   Figure 5.10

ing high points sit higher than those having low points (see Figure 5.11). Inspection of such a chart yields insights into possible problems of personnel management in the course of reorganization. For example, say the manager of manufacturing evaluates lower than the manager of engineering. If, as a means of broadening experience, it is proposed to interchange the incumbents of these two positions, special measures will have to be taken to avoid a demotivating salary downgrade for one of them, or possibly both if the interchange is then reversed after a suitable period.

On this chart we notice the long vertical line from the manager, quality control to the next lowest position, lab chief. This does not look like a conventional promotional ladder.

Long vertical lines always suggest the possibility of regrouping. For instance, the chart as a whole has a peculiar look. Here is this vice presidential position which has reporting to it a cluster of relatively low-level positions: the manager, inventory and production control; the manager, warehouses; the manager, administration; and a statistician. It looks like a daddy long-legs, and one wonders why so high a position must supervise so many routine and modest functions.

The Planner, in reviewing existing organizations, should be prepared to question exaggerated linkages of positions; and also to avoid creating new ones.

CHART ANALYSIS

Analyzing an organization chart is, of course, no more than analyzing the structure of the organization that it summarizes. The chart is merely a device for studying and altering the organization, as a mock-up model is a device for examining and changing the construc-

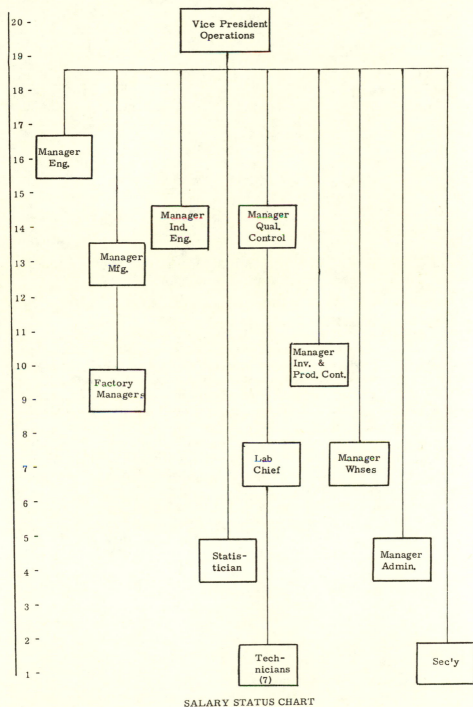

SALARY STATUS CHART

Figure 5.11

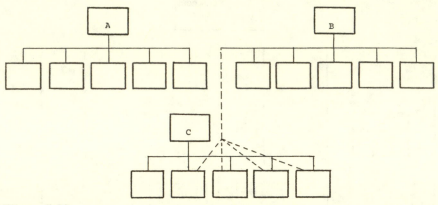

Figure 5.12

tion of a piece of machinery. A few general topics are of interest in critiquing either existing or proposed organizations.

SPAN OF ATTENTION

We sometimes hear of span of control. How many "boxes" is it safe to put under one manager on an organization chart? Before answering this, we must remember that some managers handle more positions than they directly supervise. For example, in Figure 5.12, managers A and B may each have under them five positions directly supervised or controlled. But B also has *indirect* functional direction over four other positions directly reporting to a third manager, C. Obviously B's span of *attention* is greater than the span of control. The functional supervision brings more people to keep track of. *Span of attention* is what counts.

There is no reliable rule of thumb about span, though we may be told that "the maximum span of control is seven subordinates." Under this rule, as we clamber down the organization chart from the CEO we are irresistibly reminded of the nursery rhyme:

> As I was going to St. Ives,
> I met a man with seven wives.
> Every wife had seven sacks,
> Every sack had seven cats,
> Every cat had seven kits...

This is how charts expand.

What one should do is consider the true demands of the job. Generally speaking, a manager can handle more subordinates if they are:

- All doing the same type of thing, so that the manager does not have to keep switching hats
- Doing the same thing every day, so that the manager is not chivvied by plans, decisions, instruction and follow-up
- Extremely able, so that the manager does not have to constantly watch and advise them
- In a static unchanging structure, so that the manager does not have to cope with job changes.

The manager can handle relatively fewer immediate subordinates if they are:

- Performing dissimilar, unrelated tasks
- Working on independent assignments or missions that the manager must integrate for the end results of his or her organizational unit
- Doing unstandardized, changing work requiring supervisory intervention
- In a learning situation
- In a rapidly evolving, changing environment
- Reliant on the manager for specialized or professional know-how.

How many direct subordinates can be handled also depends, obviously, on how much supporting staff is available and on how much time the manager also gives to:

- Working with his or her boss
- Personally doing tasks and assignments
- Traveling
- Dealing with outsiders
- Providing functional direction to other areas.

If the span of attention is too great, the manager will not be able to fulfill all the accountabilities of the job.

If it is too small (with only two subordinates, for example) you may wonder if the position is really a "managing" or "supervising" position at all.

Span of attention varies widely among companies. Sometimes it is dictated by circumstances, sometimes by opinion; sometimes it just happens. As an example it is interesting to look at the actual organization charts of regions of two chains of inns, which for the sake of confidentiality we will call respectively LMN Inns and OPQ Inns (see Figure 5.13). LMN Inns has a regional vice president with a staff of nine covering four widely separated districts with twenty-

Figure 5.13

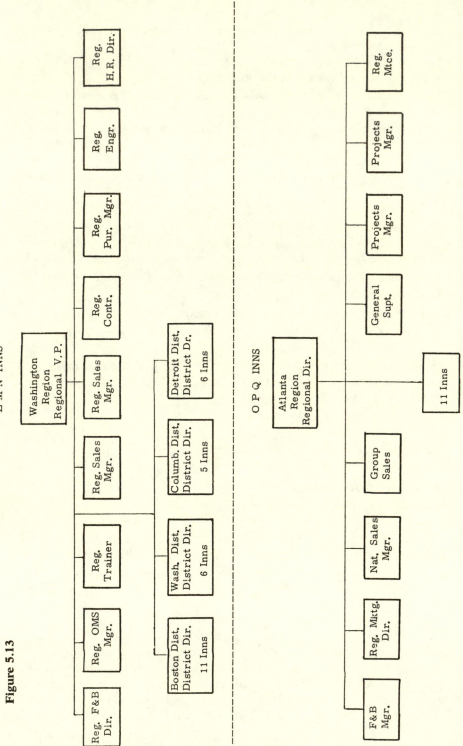

L M N INNS

```
                        ┌────────────────┐
                        │  Washington    │
                        │  Region        │
                        │  Regional V.P. │
                        └───────┬────────┘
        ┌───────┬───────┬───────┼───────┬───────┬───────┬───────┐
  ┌─────────┐┌──────┐┌────────┐┌──────┐┌──────┐┌──────┐┌──────┐┌──────┐
  │Reg. F&B ││Reg.  ││Reg.    ││Reg.  ││Reg.  ││Reg.  ││Reg.  ││Reg.  │
  │Dir.     ││OMS   ││Trainer ││Sales ││Sales ││Contr.││Pur.  ││Engr. │
  │         ││Mgr.  ││        ││Mgr.  ││Mgr.  ││      ││Mgr.  ││      │
  └─────────┘└──────┘└───┬────┘└──────┘└──────┘└──────┘└──────┘└──────┘
                                                                ┌──────┐
                                                                │Reg.  │
                                                                │H.R.  │
                                                                │Dir.  │
                                                                └──────┘
```

(Reg. Sales Mgr. branch)
- Boston Dist., District Dir. — 11 Inns
- Wash. Dist., District Dir. — 6 Inns
- Columb. Dist., District Dir. — 5 Inns
- Detroit Dist., District Dr. — 6 Inns

O P Q INNS

```
                        ┌────────────────┐
                        │  Atlanta       │
                        │  Region        │
                        │  Regional Dir. │
                        └───────┬────────┘
   ┌──────┬──────┬──────┬───────┼──────┬──────┬──────┬──────┐
┌──────┐┌──────┐┌──────┐┌──────┐   ┌──────┐┌──────┐┌──────┐┌──────┐
│F&B   ││Reg.  ││Nat.  ││Group │   │Genl. ││Projects││Projects││Reg. │
│Mgr.  ││Mktg. ││Sales ││Sales │   │Supt. ││Mgr.  ││Mgr.  ││Mtce. │
│      ││Dir.  ││Mgr.  ││      │   │      ││      ││      ││      │
└──────┘└──────┘└──────┘└──────┘   └──────┘└──────┘└──────┘└──────┘
                        │
                   ┌─────────┐
                   │ 11 Inns │
                   └─────────┘
```

eight individual locations. OPQ Inns has a regional director with a staff of eight covering eleven inns in or around a single city. In the first case the ratio of locations to top dog is 28 to 1. In the second it is 11 to 1. The ratio of locations to total supervisors (excluding staff) is in the first case 5.6 to 1; in the second, 7 to 1, not too different. LMN, however, has far less staff per location than OPQ, with more territory to cover. A reorganization Planner looking at these charts would have to wonder which is the better setup—LMN with its lower overhead or OPQ with its closer and fuller management? There is no rule of thumb. You have to get into the circumstances. Perhaps you even have to experiment a little to see how far you can extend span before running into trouble.

NOTE

1. John Dryden, "8th Book of Ovid's Metamorphoses, Meleager and Atalanta."

6

Organization Charts II

"ASSISTANTS"

The word "assistant" on the chart should always raise questions. One question is: Does the word denote an "assistant-to" or "administrative assistant"—that is, an aide having only limited authority? In this use it is often enough only a faintly prestigious term for secretary and does no harm when properly shown on the chart (see Figure 6.1).

On the other hand, an assistant in the direct line of command creates problems. Just what is the purpose of having the assistant shown in Figure 6.2?

It may be quite legitimate: the manager is on the road much of the time and the assistant manager runs the store during these absences.

But the position may not be all that it seems. Perhaps it is a safe refuge for a worthy but no longer energetic employee. Perhaps it is in reality an administrative assistant or assistant-to, misnamed. If the manager is present and managing, there seems little reason to have an intermediary to pass decisions up and down. Moreover, if it exists in one department it encourages emulation in others. "My position has a job evaluation two grades higher than my subordinates," a manager muses; "but if there were an assistant manager between me and them, my job might move up a grade." "Jones has an assistant manager under him, and I don't," another tells his wife; "it seems to build his position a little higher than mine, if you know what I mean." "That guy Smith under me is always crying for a promotion," thinks another; "and I don't want to lose him, but he's certainly not getting

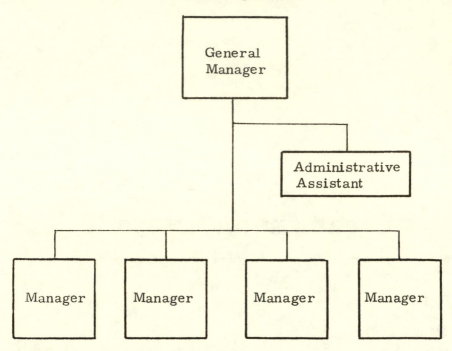

Figure 6.1

my job. Maybe if I were to let him keep on doing what he's doing, but name him 'assistant manager'...."

The last ploy calls attention to yet another problem. For every incumbent of a position there should be at least two identifiable replacements in case the position becomes vacant. But an assistant manager seems to have a lock on the boss's job. What if there's a better candidate somewhere else?

LEVELS

That there should not be "too many levels" is an article of faith with some critics of the management scene. "The president should not be more than seven levels removed from the sweeper" is a typical dictum. Just why this should be is hard to say. Is it meant to encourage folksiness? To make things happen faster?

The heads of many well-run companies never see the workers on the factory floor or in the back office. They do not have time to. And organizations are often of a size that makes the supervision of large numbers of people impossible without multiple levels. It is as though you were to say that a staircase should never have more than seven steps.

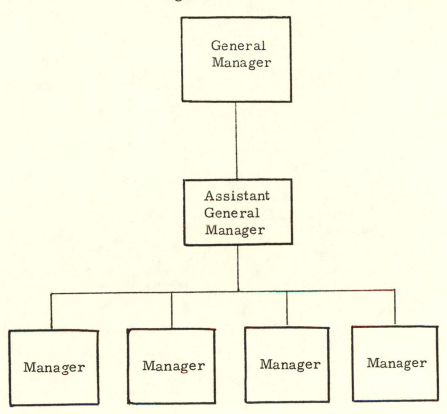

Figure 6.2

On the other hand, multiple levels often creep in where they are not needed. In Figure 6.3 we have three interpositions of managers between real manager and real operatives. Everything in this chart looks neat and orderly, but the skeptic may ask: What do those managers do all day long? Do they make managerial decisions or merely pass information up and down?

And here is a sales organization in Figure 6.4. That manager, sales regions—what is the position's function? Is it a relay station between the east and west region managers and the general manager of sales, handing messages and reports back and forth? Why not have the two regions report directly to the general manager? It looks very much like a chart with an extra level.

More than that, here is a one-over-two position, always open to challenge. A truly managerial position should be able to manage more than two subordinates. There are, of course, exceptions. An apparently one-over-two may bracket an additional number of indirectly supervised positions, though that does not seem to be the case here.

Figure 6.3

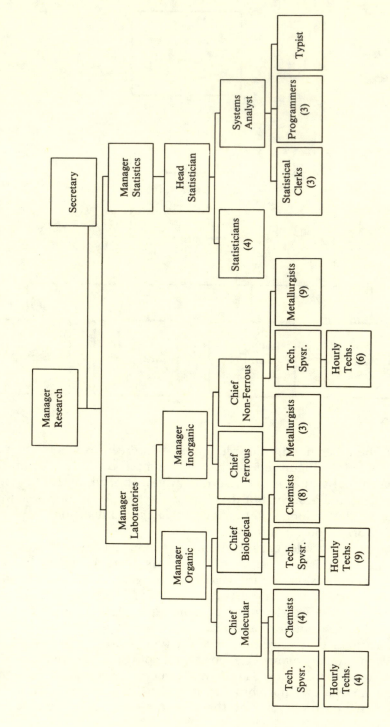

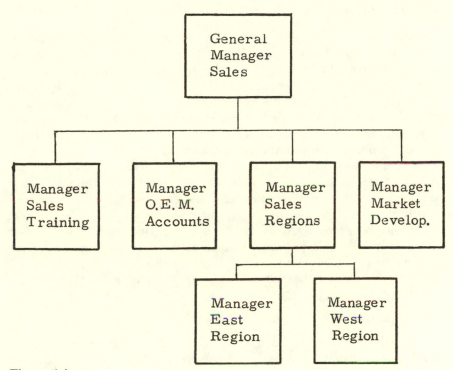

Figure 6.4

It may, especially in our sales example, be preoccupied with calling on major accounts, in which case it is less of a manager, more of an upper-level ambassador. But its appearance as both a redundant level and a transmitter rather than a manager raises questions as to its necessity. Similar superfluities can be found in many areas of an organization, set up for the sake of symmetry, recognition of superior ability, or technical rather than managerial performance. Often they are dispensable. They are not only costly, they retard communication and action. They create too many chiefs per Indian.

Some companies destratify themselves. Of DuPont Company, for example, it is reported that "at headquarters, management layers have been reduced and responsibility pushed downward. Departments that had two vice presidents now have one or none. Plants have four levels of supervision instead of seven or eight. Newly liberated middle managers talk enthusiastically of exercising 'broader spans of control.' "[1] You do not know how much managers can handle until you challenge them.

PROMOTIONAL LINES

Some attempt should be made to avoid what may be called desert island jobs, stuck off by themselves with little opportunity for escape. For example, consider Figure 5.11 in the previous chapter. The statistician reports, doubtless for good reasons, to the vice president. But it's a dead-end job. There's nothing above it to be promoted to. It builds no managerial experience. Dead-end jobs should be avoided. They sooner or later dissatisfy an able incumbent. Worse, they deprive the company of promotional candidates.

Now it is true that not every employee, particularly not every specialist, qualifies or even hankers for promotion. But the chartist is not a personality analyst. Properly placing positions in the lower reaches of the chart means providing a ladder for those incumbents who may be encouraged to climb to better things. Jobs hitched to the end of a long rope should be eschewed unless there are clear opportunities for lateral transfer.

The organization chart should support the eligibility chart.

NORMAL STAFFING

Just what constitutes normal staffing in the company? Consider a company that may just possibly be overstaffed because it follows an unvoiced policy of always having enough people to take care of any contingency. For example, Accounts Payable carries enough clerks to handle the surge of business at the turn of the month. There are enough factory electricians to take care of occasional installation work as well as normal maintenance. The typing pool is ready for any special workload imposed by lengthy reports and statements.

As an alternative, a more conscious policy might direct that the number of employees be only sufficient to conduct the day-in-day-out events of the business. For example, the *Wall Street Journal* reported that the Continental Illinois Corp. of Chicago (on a campaign unrelated to its subsequent difficulties), set up "a cadre of part-time help for peak-time loads to assist fewer full-timers in areas like check-processing."[2] Some factories carry a building maintenance force sufficient to take care of ordinary repairs but call in outside contractors to put on a new roof or repave the driveway. In architectural and construction offices there may be rows of empty drafting tables, to be filled by short-term draftspersons only when a big contract is snared.

Some forms of work-force management are so idiosyncratic, and incidentally successful, that they are virtually inconceivable to the managements of permanent-work-force enterprises. Consider a competent motion picture producer, who assembles a diverse crew of artists, accountants, directors, grips, carpenters, camera operators, cafeteria managers, designers, and technicians, manages them superbly through a predetermined budget and time-frame, and then, having completed the manufacture of a movie, disbands the whole outfit. Or in a wholly different field, consider the consortiums that were formed to put up the World Trade Center buildings, then, mission accomplished, dissolved. If such special-purpose feats can be accomplished on a large scale, cannot smaller ones be achieved in the more conventional company or institution?

Instead of retaining permanent staff for any contingency, the company may rely on a host of available external personnel: retirees, terminated former employees, "ex's" who have resigned for personal reasons (such as raising a family), free lancers, school and college teachers, relatives of employees, and of course, temporary help services. Even the employment application files may yield candidates for part-time work.

Understaffing is easy to correct. Overstaffing, on the other hand, wastes resources. And it is not easy to recognize, for few managers will confess to it. The Planner must try to detect if it exists through a developing sense of company norms derived from personal contact with many managers.

THE WHOLE CHART

So much attention—perhaps nit-picking attention—to the details of chart construction should not divert us from the chart's real message. The chart is not an end in itself—it is but the projected shadow of a real body of people. The Planner, consulting with various executives on the best ways to group positions, is dealing with how those people direct their efforts to products, customers, and finances. Are they apt to succeed in these efforts? For a clue it is important to consider the chart as a whole.

Not everyone believes this. For example, Professor H. Edward Wrapp at the Graduate School of Business, University of Chicago has told us that "preoccupation with...comprehensive organization charts and job descriptions—this is often the first symptom of an organization which is in the early stages of atrophy."[3] Says Robert Townsend in *Up The Organization* under the heading "Organization Charts: Rigor Mortis," "They have uses....But draw them in pencil. Never formalize, print, or circulate them. Good organizations are living bodies that grow new muscles to meet challenges....In the best organizations people see themselves working in a circle as if around one table."[4] Harlan Cleveland, former Assistant Secretary of State, has told us that "the organizations that get things done will no longer be hierarchical pyramids with most of the real content at the top. They will be *systems*—interlaced webs of tension in which control is loose, power is diffused, and centers of decision are plural."[5] I need hardly say that in admirable Japan, organizations are so porous that everyone does everything. When a visitor buys a defective disc player at the Odakyu Department Store, who comes to replace it—a customer relations clerk? Oh, no: Odakyu's vice president, along with a junior employee. "Three minutes after the exhausted pair arrived they were climbing back into the waiting cab," the reporter, Hilary Hinds Kitasei, tells us.[6] Doubtless they had to get back to pitch in on washing the store windows. And Alvin Toffler, peering into the future, sees the arrival of new kinds of organizations, doubtless chartless, that will be free and open: "Instead of being trapped in some unchanging, personality-smashing niche, man will find himself liberated, a stranger in a new, free-form world of kinetic organizations. In this landscape, his position will be constantly changing, fluid, and varied."[7]

This is all very nice, and if there is a flaw in this almost Marxist, almost, for goodness' sake, *anarchist* vision of a band of people all doing their own and everybody else's thing, freed from the artificial hedgerows of the organization chart—if there is a flaw, it lies in the fact that they are human beings and as such expect, nay crave, organization. Suppose for example, that we were to take our chart (Figure 5.4) and utterly abolish all those hateful levels and lines of authority and separation (see Figure 6.5). We would have only a group of peopled positions floating freely like motes in a sunbeam, "working in a circle," as Townsend only too aptly put it. This is a way to run a business?

One thing that may happen is that a pecking order will establish itself. This may not lead the company in the direction that it would like to go, if we may draw parallels from the animal world. Dr. Alison Jolly of Rockefeller University cites studies of rhesus monkeys which indicate that "dominant males performed worse than other males on several types of learning and reasoning tasks. . . . Dominant males are less likely than others to take up new habits."[8] Or as Bergen Evans has said, "Leadership is more likely to be assumed by the aggressive than by the able, and those who scramble to the top are more often motivated by their own inner torments than by any demand for their guidance."[9] Free-for-all management carries its risks. (But then, so does conventional management. No one requires executives to pass ability tests, the way a mail carrier, for example, does.)

Chartless organization may even be deceptive, for there are still unseen networks connecting people. Other webs could easily be su-

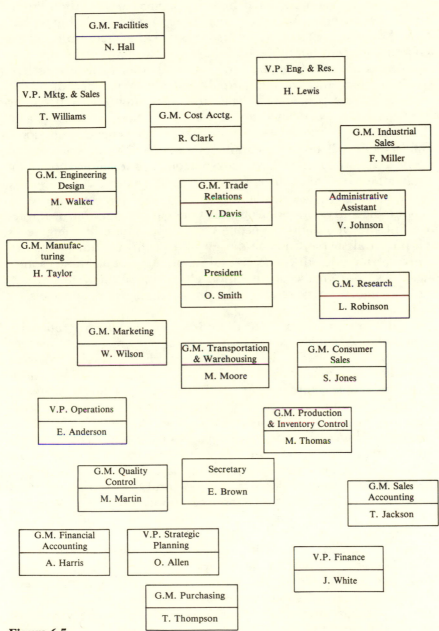

Figure 6.5

perimposed on the mass, for behind the formal organization lie informal ones by no means ineffective. There are uncharted networks of employees who belong to lodges, to bowling leagues, to religious denominations, to family relationships, to car pools. Affinities and oppositions abound. Organization occurs whether we will it or not. Even the disorganization of Figure 6.5 is transitory; a pecking order is bound to emerge and verticalize it. So we might as well try for order consciously dedicated to the company's needs; the chart as a whole must serve the company's purposes. Things have to get done. Someone has to hand out assignments, someone has to decide whom to hire and how to let someone go, someone has to control spending within allowable limits, someone has to see that work is done properly and well, someone has to visualize results, and someone has to be accountable for results. Someone has to assemble even the most free-form interactive groups. Someone has to coordinate fifty engineers and fifty draftspersons in the design of a product, someone has to motivate and guide the scattered salesmen. Are not all these "someones" positions on the organization chart, hierarchic and bureaucratic though it may seem? ("Hierarchy, a division of angels"—Webster's.[10])

Is it not indeed possible that there is an innate human propensity for organizing, manifested not only in the arrangement of a business enterprise but in many other fields as well? For example, Professor Erwin Panofsky describes the analogies between medieval scholasticism and medieval architecture: "The formalism of Scholastic writing reached its climax in the classic *Summa* with its three requirements of (1) totality (sufficient enumeration), (2) arrangement according to a system of homologous parts and parts of parts (sufficient articulation), and (3) distinctness and deductive cogency (sufficient interrelation). . . . We take it for granted that major works of scholarship, especially systems of philosophy and doctoral theses, are organized according to a scheme of division and subdivision." And later on, speaking of the great cathedrals, he says that "this principle of progressive divisibility (or to look at it the other way, multiplicability) increasingly affected the entire edifice down to the smallest detail. At the height of the development, supports were divided and subdivided into main piers, major shafts, minor shafts, and still minor shafts; the tracery of windows, triforia, and blind arcades into primary, secondary, and tertiary mullions and profiles."[11] Why, it all sounds very much like today's company organization chart, even down to its "multiplicability." Hierarchies come naturally to us, passed down over the centuries, and trying to dicerp them in a company may be the equivalent of proposing to tear down a cathedral.

The true problem is not whether to have an organization chart. It is: What should the chart represent? We can deal with its details, its one-over-twos, and its multiple levels, but how do we approach it as a whole? Are we dealing with reality or with conventional artificiality?

It has occurred to a number of people that management, far from being realistic, is really mythbound. H. Edward Wrapp lists five "myths ... widely held notions" that "permeate the literature on management:"

- Life gets less complicated as a manager reaches the top of the pyramid.
- The manager at the top level knows everything that's going on in the organization, can command whatever resources he may need, and therefore can be more decisive.
- The general manager's day is taken up with making broad policy decisions and formulating precise objectives.
- The top executive's primary activity is conceptualizing long-range plans.
- In a large company, the top executive may be seen meditating about the role of his organization in society.[12]

Henry Mintzberg, a professor at McGill University, has discovered four other myths:

Myth 1: The manager is a reflective, systematic planner....

Myth 2: The effective manager has no duties to perform....

Myth 3: The senior manager needs aggregated information, which a formal management information system best provides....

Myth 4: Management is, or at least is quickly becoming, a science and a profession.[13]

These myths are mentioned here not because of their substance, though it is certainly thought-provoking, but because they raise a general question. What specific myths govern the reorganization of a particular company? Sometimes it is the company's supposed policies that are the myths.

On the whole, policy is a boon to management. It need not originate with management and be foisted on underlings. It may arise from a consensus of those on the firing line: the assembly workers may among themselves, for example, evolve a policy of permitting no defective work to reach the inspectors.

The more the employees are guided by policy, the fewer the decisions that have to travel up the line. This is fine, and by reducing managerial workload should reduce the need for managers, if decision making has been much of their job. How prevalent policy is can shape structure.

But suppose there are other company myths that bear on the organization and its chart. For example, the myths that we just quoted plus other more immediate ones, such as:

- No customer is too small to be dealt with.
- No purchases are made except on the basis of at least three bids.
- No action is taken without consensus.
- The more communication, the better the performance.
- No product change affecting quality is made without the president's approval.
- Electronic data processing is preferable to any alternative.
- No manager should do what could be done by a subordinate.

Some of these may be policies, others only beliefs. A reorganization might introduce another: the more that people do their own thing and do it well, the less the need for communication. In fact the more they do their own thing on their own, the better they will do it. But this is true only in some companies. And where it is not true, no overnight organization chart change will make it come true.

It is difficult to recognize intraorganizational myths for what they are. We may spot the obvious ones without being aware that others even exist, just as pre-Copernican astronomers may have understood that constellations were a sort of myth without ever supposing that geocentricity was anything but a self-evident fact and not a myth too.

All the same, when considering an organization chart the viewer, having eliminated small glitches, may ask: what company myths can be smoked out? Are any of them responsible for this chart's complexity? Is a corrective process available to make the organization and its chart more compact? For example, timestudy may determine how many heads and pairs of hands are needed at the chart's bottom line, and custom usually determines that only one person sits at the top of the chart; but what says how many bosses and experts are needed in between? You can try various approaches:

- Try to identify company myths that bloat the chart.
- Check out spans of attention and levels.
- Try overloading bosses by combining positions; it may force a relinquishment of expensive "nothing" tasks at inappropriate levels.
- Extend policy guidance so that fewer decisions move to upper levels for time-consuming review and approval.
- Combine functions in order to reduce the need for costly and unnoticed communication.
- Simplify company systems before embalming them in the computer.
- Get rid of all bosses, in the happy commune spirit.

No, forget the last item. It won't result from a reorganization. If you're starting up a new organization—say a new factory or office— you may specify the climate it will be born in and shape the organization, if any, accordingly. But changing the climate of an existing organization is a longish process, and any organization changes are more apt to follow than precede it. The other approaches are worth considering, for they may contribute to better performance.

No matter what the specific objective of reorganization—a switch from function to product orientation, for example—there is always the hope that along with it will flow a reduction in expense or cost. This in itself represents a form of better performance. And often with it is allied tighter, more effective, faster-reacting control. So as part of the overall approaches to reorganization we may add to our list one more:

• Consider reducing the number of departments.

This brings us back to Buck Gray's company, where George Brown has been succeeded by Jim Green, the new president.

NOTES

1. *Wall Street Journal*, 25 Sept. 1985.

2. *Wall Street Journal*, 29 Mar. 1983.

3. H. Edward Wrapp, "Good Managers Don't Make Policy Decisions," *Harvard Business Review* (July-August 1984; reprinted from *Harvard Business Review*, September-October 1967), pp. 8, 12.

4. Robert Townsend, *Up The Organization* (New York: Alfred A. Knopf, 1970), p. 134.

5. Harlan Cleveland, "The Decision Makers," *The Center Magazine* (September-October 1973):p. 11.

6. *Wall Street Journal*, 30 July 1985.

7. Alvin Toffler, *Future Shock* (New York: Bantam Books, 1970), p. 124.

8. Alison Jolly, "The Evolution of Primate Behavior," *American Scientist* (May-June 1985): p. 230.

9. Bergen Evans, *The Spoor of Spooks and Other Nonsense* (New York: Alfred A. Knopf, 1954).

10. *Webster's Seventh New Collegiate Dictionary*, s. v. "hierarchy."

11. Erwin Panofsky, *Gothic Architecture and Scholasticism* (Cleveland and New York: Meridian Books, The World Publishing Company, 1968), pp. 31, 48.

12. Wrapp, "Good Managers," p. 8.

13. Henry Mintzberg, "The Manager's Job: Folklore and Fact," *Harvard Business Review* (July–August 1975).

7

Departmental Analysis I

One of the first things Green does after coming aboard as president is put a hold on the Deaf Smith shutdown. "Small plants aren't all bad," he says. "Often they can make and ship at lower cost than a giant one. Also, under the right kind of supervision a small factory can be like a big family. You don't have to worry about setting up quality circles. They're built in. Let's keep it open."

"On the other hand," Green muses, "we do seem to have a surfeit of departments. Making unnecessary trips to factories and warehouses. Throwing blocks on their own teammates instead of on the competition. Gobbling up money before it can drop into the after-tax slot. In fact . . ."

ORGANIZATION THERAPY

Over the next months Green devotes himself to sculpting a sparer company departmental structure. "Like chipping away at the stone to get at the statue within," he tells the chairman of the board. First he designates for elimination any department providing a service that can be more efficiently produced outside. "We're expert in making plastic hardware," he says, "but we're wasting time and money trying to manage a hundred things we're not expert at—like, for instance," he points to an organization chart, "trying to run an in-house print shop."

The print shop goes. With it goes the main die shop, whose departing employees buy up the machine tools they had formerly run, set up an independent business, and underbid the very jobs they used to work on. Green now considers a new-generation computer that has taken four hours being "presented" to him with slides and flip charts. "What if we put the whole thing out for bid to service bureaus?" he asks. "Let them be experts on computing and we'll be experts in making and selling our goods and managing our money." ("He may be right," the controller says later to his assistant, "but at least he can't move on it very fast." "And a good thing, too. We've got the office football pool loaded into that thing. You'd have rioting in the halls.") During the presentation Green has caught a reference to a program that has just been prepared for the pension fund management department. "Why not switch to outside professionals in the field?" he wonders, and another flake of stone falls away.

But Green has not only been shifting functions out from within the company. Brown's housecleaning had left many small, underpopulated, overworked departments, each with its own manager and budget. Those that he has not eliminated Green now regroups into larger ones.

Sometimes he gets welcome feedback. "Hey, Green," a customer says on the phone. "Just wanted you to know we appreciate whatever it is you're doing there. Since you cut two weeks from your order processing time we've been able to lower our order points and reduce our inventories. I call that good news." "Yeah, thanks," Green responds. "Now for the bad news. We've speeded up some other things and you're going to be getting your invoice the same day you get our shipment, not a week later like it used to be when it took three departments to get it mailed." "Go ahead. We'll be paying with a check drawn on a bank in Anchorage. Any other changes coming up?" Green has not mentioned, though he is sure his customer knows, that in one sales region he is experimenting with manufacturers' reps as a substitute for the sales force, so that more executive time can go to customers rather than internal management.

Through what is left of the grapevine comments and jokes work their way back to Green. But he does not care. "We've cut down our managerial bulge," he explains to his staff. "But more importantly, we've reduced interdepartmental forms (Brown's bugaboo), letters, phone calls, travel, conferences, territorial squabbling, and even (thinking of the pension fund program) the load on our computers, or on the people who will supply computer services. And the fewer departments, the fewer approvals and the less time lost as everything inches from desk to desk. Our problem wasn't making decisions, it was executing them. One of our plant managers could decide to buy a lift truck, but he couldn't get it bought. As someone said, too many cooks don't spoil the broth, they just never get it to the table."

"I don't know," says one of the vice presidents, candid because near retirement. "To my mind you're taking away all control. Who's going to ride herd on the factories and warehouses and sales districts, just for the company's protection?"

"Control? What am I paying Gray and all the other field managers for? He's a competent adult. We give him an expense budget, an inventory budget, and a capital budget and beyond that I trust his judgment. If he has enough sense to manage a five million dollar payroll, he's got enough to buy a lift truck. The owner of an independent factory runs his own show. Why not Gray?"

And "Why not," Green might have said, "me?" For Green has accomplished what few CEOs have. He has got inside of his organization. Not content with its hand-me-down departmental ornamentation, he has deliberately defurnished it so that its "sightlines," as he calls them, are clear and unobstructed. Combining unnecessarily fragmented functions, he has shortened paths of communication. He has clarified and pinpointed accountability. He has thrust out of the company all activities that competing suppliers can do better than internal hacks. All this he has done and made secure against relapse by eliminating departments rather than merely individuals. And this, he reflects, may even have its humanitarian aspects. Better for a job-hunter to be able to think, "my department was eliminated," than, "I was singled out. Why me?"

DEPARTMENTALISM

In our example departments are by their nature consumers of company energies. Is it possible that departmentalism, necessary though it is, can distort an organization, thwart its purposes, waste its money, frustrate its employees, or disaffect its customers? How can it be exploited, assessed, rearranged, and improved? These are some of the questions this chapter proposes to address. For departmentalism, by partitioning a company, can set it at cross-purposes with as much detriment as any competitive threat. It can, however, be dealt with.

Examining and appraising departments as such, rather than their constituent members, may uncover potential for improvement in profit and organizational effectiveness. To illustrate, I propose to describe some of the problems of cost and performance that departments themselves can cause. I will also suggest ways to deal with them.

COST DILATION

Departmentalization—and by department I mean any subdivision of the organization, whether it is called a division, a department, a section, a bureau, an "office", a shop, or any of the other terms that bedevil structuralists trying to devise distinctions—departmentalization, inescapable as it is, introduces often unchallenged costs that can be shrunk by desupervising, consolidating, and decolonizing.

DESUPERVISING

First, of course, is the cost of managers. Obviously, the more departments, the more supervisors and managers. Some do productive work. Others, bare-desk executives making small decisions and passing out assignments, may be little more than high-paid, well-titled equivalents of the dispatcher at the local freight terminal. "I have an aversion to titles," says Harry A. Merlo, chairman and president of Louisiana-Pacific. "You give a guy a title and he hires someone to do his job."[1] Too many departments means too many titles and supervisors which means too much payroll.

In current pare-back times the problem may arise without being recognized. Consider the firm which, unable to earn profits through its primary purpose of selling goods and services to customers at a reasonable price, turns to an alternative: dispeopling the company. As employees march through the exit interviews, what is left may be departmental husks almost emptied of their contents. The company winds up talent-poor, department-rich. And the heavy end of the payroll remains—managers. Why not shrink the structure as well as the work force?

For example, one medium-sized company found, after a cutback, that it was left with a training department and an art department, each having a supervisor and no employees; a two-person employment department; and several small financial analysis departments scattered among divisions, each with its own "manager." It then took the further step of eliminating the first two altogether, relying instead on outside services as needed. It absorbed the employment function into a larger personnel group and consolidated the financial analysis elements into the controller's staff. By thus "desupervising" it lowered its overall supervisory cost per employee (always a statistic worth checking throughout the company).

CONSOLIDATING

This company also saved more than the mere cost of managers who have few to supervise. For supervision is not the only cost borne by companies aswarm with departments. A second burden is what might be called "running costs." Every separate department has its own set of files (regardless of the central file, in which things tend to be hard to locate). It is included in other departments' mailing lists, and in turn types and issues communiqués of its own. It gets its own computer printouts, for which it must have its own storage cabinets. Its members sit in on meetings and they take trips. It devotes time to preparing its budget, with appropriate safety padding. It hoards its stock of office sundries. Small staff departments cost more in the aggregate than many large ones. By their mere existence they run up costs.

If this is the case in offices, are factory departments any different? Seldom. For example, in many factories each department must perforce duplicate what every other has. Let there be a screw-machine department, an engine lathe department, a drilling department, a shaper department, and a milling department, and each has not only its own supervisor but also its own setup mechanic, repair mechanic, sweeper, material handler, and clerk, all for the best reasons. It may even have its own cache of inventory, ex-stockroom, ready to feed in when an interruption or shortage occurs. All this is just excess running cost, overdepartmentalization's impost. Why put up with it when the cure is consolidation?

As a large scale example, one steel company having two nearby mills put them under joint general supervision. Result: one superintendent's office where before there were two, one accounting department, one engineering department, and one metallurgical department.

"In slimming its payroll," says the *Wall Street Journal*, "Wells Fargo closed 13 of its 397 branches (while adding three others), pulled consumer-loan makers out of branches and consolidated them centrally, reduced publications and dropped its real-estate-appraisal department."[2]

On a smaller scale, an appliance manufacturer having acquired another in the same field, chose not to continue all the separate staff departments of the acquired firm. Instead it discontinued them and picked up the work in its existing departments; and while retaining an assembly facility in the original location for distribution economies, it closed down the machining and stamping departments, accommodating them in its already available shop capacity. Thus a contraction in the number of departments permitted outright savings.

A major electrical manufacturer reorganized four corporate-wide divisions into three. Same work, fewer departments.

For another example, within five months of becoming CEO of Norwest [banking] Corporation, Lloyd P. Johnson said that, "We're going to centralize every function we can legally, in an attempt to use the separate banks as marketing offices, with processing, asset-liability management and product design handled by the holding company." "He noted that Norwest currently uses eight operating centers to process checks and other transactions, while Security Pacific [a competitor] has been able to consolidate nearly all of that activity at a single plant outside Los Angeles, cutting its costs."[3]

What these examples illustrate is the need for going after big chunks, not just little pieces, of the cost problem. Job-by-job or function-by-function analysis is of undoubted value. It boots a few squatters out of the tenement, so to speak, and for a while the place is more habitable. But more enduring is redesign of the structure itself, with emphasis on eliminating those cubicles that add to its cost of upkeep; namely, departments.

DECOLONIZING

A third cost of departmental proliferation comes from doing inside what can be done better by outside specialists. Quaker Oats Company, for example, for sixteen years had its own in-house ad agency, with seventy-two employees. It sold it off to Backer & Spielvogel, whose main business is advertising, not cereal manufacture.[4]

Many companies support service departments that are unrelated to the main business. Originally, convenience and supposed low cost led to the establishment of such enclaves. Today these may be outweighed by the technical limitations and high overhead of their continuance. Thus a steel mill closed down its pattern shop and an electrical goods manufacturer discontinued its foundry, going to outside suppliers and finding that access to more up-to-date equipment, greater schedule flexibility, and simplification of internal management yielded significant savings. Not just in the wages of the employees but in the pure nuisance cost of being distracted by unnecessary, obsolete, marginal departments is where the savings lay.

Purging the company of small specialist departments has several benefits.

- It relieves upper management of the time spent keeping track of, supervising, and budgeting these small colonies in the organization structure.
- It saves operating expense, especially when company wage scale and benefits are being paid for jobs that can be done at lower cost by outside suppliers.
- It reduces investment in and upkeep of internal facilities and the space they occupy.
- It saves on direct supervisory costs.
- It often provides higher-skilled, more up-to-date, more adaptable service from those who specialize in it on a large scale.

The company sells its goods and services in a free market. Let it buy the same way, and get rid of inside monopolies.

PERFORMANCE

Out and out, up-front, highly visible cost is not the only mischief created by overdepartmentalization. More subtle is internal degradation of performance. It dogs the company that is subdivided into a hive of specialized principalities. Overdepartmentalization:

- Introduces unnecessary activities—superfluous "approvals," for example, as we saw in Buck Gray's case
- Puts too many hands on the steering wheel, slowing down reaction time, skewing the business' forward thrust
- Creates confusion by separating functions that should be handled jointly
- Holds the business back by paradoxically depriving it of skills more available elsewhere
- Creates a communications mentality that preoccupies departments with "telling" rather than "doing"
- Multiplies clerical activities
- Enlarges the theater of guerrilla fighting.

Let me illustrate.

APPROVALITIS

A company can strangle in its own middle management.

In our forklift example, the company is obviously suffering from approvalitis. Nothing can be done without an imprimatur from every possible remotely concerned department. Many departments means many approvals. And the more approvals, the greater the project time as the paperwork waits for attention. Are these approvals even needed? Who required them in the first place? Probably the very departments involved. One company, concerned by the long lead time between conception and first delivery of sales promotions, examined the eleven approvals on each marketing appropriation. Of these it found that four were genuine *I approve*'s and the rest were *I am informed*'s. But the documents were spending weeks on the approval circuit. To reduce the lead time it therefore cut the approval blocks on the appropriation form to four, all the other interested departments receiving advisory copies with five days for objection to any project that would cause problems. As a result the lead time was truncated to a third of its former length. If there must be departments, let them not be impediments.

OVERPARTICIPATION

Staff departments, given too much rein, can eat up the time of operating ones, to the company's detriment. We saw an example of this in our opening case, where the plant manager, Gray, was being assailed with questions and advice on dock plates and fuels. All this to-and-fro discourse is more than an annoyance. It diverts his time from his plant to his desk. It also, of course, provides staff busy-work. But what does this contribute to the company's success in selling at a profit?

The solution to this type of overparticipation is the policy that line managers bear responsibility for what they do. With policy as a gyro-compass to keep on course, you do not need a host of departments squinting at the binnacle with every gust of wind, and advising the helmsman how to swing the wheel. In our example much of the interplay would have been shrunk by a simple policy: "The plant manager is fully responsible for reasonable measures for (1) meeting budget; and (2) ensuring the safety and legal compliance of the plant, operations, and employees." In support of this policy, staff departments may provide information to the manager for his assistance and may on request make periodic checkups. They may even issue sub-policies in the interests of uniformity. For example, "It is company policy that all forklift trucks be powered by propane [or gasoline or storage batteries, as the case may be] in order to facilitate transfer of vehicles between factories." By putting ad hoc decisions at the action level, policy curtails the extent of departmental meddling. It also frees up time at the "front". In our example, Gray should have been held responsible for proper decisions on his own.

A still more direct way to reduce overparticipation is simply to minimize the number of participating departments. As a drastic example, Hisao Tsubouchi, upon acquiring the Sasebo shipyards in Japan, not only reduced staff but while doing so "cut the number of work sections from 230 to eight; the result, he says, is that decisions could be made more quickly because managers weren't getting in each other's way."[5]

OVERDIFFERENTIATION

Yet another slower-upper in companies having too many departments is the separation of related functions. With overdifferentiation of duties nothing is ever finished. Done partly by one department it is laid down to be picked up by another. In our opening example the forklift was never treated as a unit. Rather it was dealt with as the blind men dealt with the elephant, a piece at a time.

Can such difficulties be corrected? Yes, by integrating. For example, at one time commercial banks customarily had a new business division and also a loan division. The first called on customers to drum up loans; the second, to work out the details and conclude the transaction. This entailed repetition, nuisance, and loss of time for all those involved. Some banks then tried training salesmen to both originate and conclude a loan on the spot. The manifest advantages to the customer and hence to the bank made it obvious that the two divisions could be combined. As a result banks were able to transfer personnel to other positions, a savings; but more importantly, the whole transaction was simplified and accelerated.

Collapsing complementary departments into one not only slims the organization, it speeds up its reflexes as well.

UNDERQUALIFICATION

A department formed in the past to provide a necessary service may in time become more of a stumbling block than a stepping stone. This is particularly true when external technology has advanced far beyond the department's affordable staff or facilities. Yet the department remains in place, underperforming though doing its best, sometimes supplementing itself with outside professional services that only magnify its own cost. At this point some companies have raised the question: Is this department any longer justifiable? And having got this far they take the further step of closing down the supererogatory department entirely in favor of purchased professionalism. For example:

- A large steel company discontinued its internal machine shop. Outside job shops, equipped with numerically-controlled tools, could do the work faster, better, and with a far wider spectrum of available skills.

- A medium-sized bank turned all its stock transfer operations over to a depository trust company, which had the software and personnel that a small trust department could not support.

- A number of processing companies have assigned research work to university and commercial laboratories, better staffed and equipped than small internal ones.

Cost savings alone did not guide these decisions. The governing factor was the companies' recognition that new technologies had made certain internal departments obsolete.

OVERCOMMUNICATION

Unfortunately no department, like no man, is an island, "intire of it selfe." Departments, particularly "office" ones, tend to communicate with one another, often in writing. This of course is not all bad. Business communications have a long and honorable history, as mounds of cuneiform tablets from disinterred Babylon attest. But before we go the way of Babylon, we might ask, can a company, or for that matter a civilization, die from impaction of the in-basket? Will copy-machinitis become a recognized disease?

Departments necessarily demand one another's attention and may well perform a necessary service for others. At the same time, by their very existence they set up communications requirements with them. Suppose, for example, that the time seems to have come to form—oh, let us say—a statutory compliance department and pull together a lot of separate pieces scattered throughout the organization. That new department then creates a whole new set of forms to be printed, stocked, filled out, passed around, possibly read, and filed. As a next step systems people move in and transfer this information, at some cost, to the computer, though this does not guarantee that the department will not still file its paper forms for easy reference. The new department issues bulletins, letters, and memorandums for other departments to take home in their briefcases before loading into their own files. It is in turn added to their mailing lists, something which might not have happened in the good old days of carbon paper. It requires an additional signature block on all appropriation requests; the passage of such requests is then slowed down one week. It occasionally mislays and holds up important correspondence. (I should explain that I am not attributing all this to "Statutory Compliance" as such; any office department will do.) It perhaps relies on documents rather than direct action to get things done ("What do you mean no one told you? You had it right there in writing, didn't you?")

Where there is a department there is a communications entrepôt. And of course communication is the great desideratum of modern business society. Colleges grant degrees in it and consultants hold seminars to push its merits. But an overdepartmentalized company risks all the costs—worse, all the malfunctions—that can accompany passing messages over walls. Our opening example, though perhaps extreme, illustrates the overcommunications problems of many departments trying to "relate." Some of the effects are:

- Too many messages
- Too many approvals
- Too many (often duplicated) records and files

- Too much time to read, interpret, and respond
- Too many delays as information inches from department to department
- Too much misunderstanding due to interface obtusity
- Just perhaps—too much office equipment.

"No problem," someone says. "Electronic mail will take care of all of this." But what will occur if it should instead multiply communications? Communications gridlock?

Many companies—and for that matter, the federal government—have mounted campaigns to reduce their volume of printed forms. These are vain efforts. A form is, after all, a more efficient communication than a letter. The real culprits are the departments that issue them. Only by consolidating, eliminating, or severely restricting departments can the communications flood be contained. The gains are two-fold: first in the department that must devote hours to their preparation and issuance and second in the time of those who, like our friend Buck Gray, must read and respond to them.

NOTES

1. *Wall Street Journal*, 19 Aug. 1982.
2. *Wall Street Journal*, 29 Mar. 1983.
3. *Wall Street Journal*, 22 July 1985.
4. *New York Times*, 10 June 1985.
5. *Wall Street Journal*, 10 Jan. 1983.

8

Departmental Analysis II

CLERICAL DUPLICATION

Another characteristic of overdepartmentalization is duplication of effort. For one example, let several departments be dealing with the same subject matter and they will often be found keeping multiple, not always consistent, records of it. Thus:

- In a manufacturing company separate finished goods inventory records were maintained by Accounting, Warehousing, Sales, Production Scheduling, and the individual factories. The records did not always agree; sometimes they showed different tallies for the same product. The solution: uniform, faster, and more available printouts from the computer. The result: clerical savings and also (and perhaps more important) elimination of misunderstanding as to what the amount of inventory really is.

- In a company with some 6,000 employees, employee listings were filed on separate tapes for the employment department, the employee communications department, the pension department, the insurance department, and the payroll department. Each contained its own set of errors. Additionally the sales and manufacturing departments each kept listings of their own employees. And the tapes themselves were supplemented with card files. The solution: a consolidation of records in one tape, with parts accessible (as appropriate) to all. The result: again, elimination of time-wasting inconsistencies and multiple entries.

Clearly, these abuses are correctible with a systems unification. But they reflect, equally clearly, the propensity of departments to duplicate one another's work if unchecked.

HUMAN FACTORS

Are not all the problems I have mentioned attributable in the end to the human failings of supervisors rather than to departments as such? Not always. Departments come to have a personality of their own that can transcend a succession of supervisors. Even in a small company they can bring vexations of cost and performance. I will not dwell on this, for the field was amply covered by the Organization Development movement some years ago, but it is worth looking at.

Something is wrong with departments that:

- Are hostile to other departments
- Are hostile even to customers
- Require others to comply with rigid procedures
- Are overdeliberate in providing service
- Have a tradition of treating their own employees either better or worse than others in the company
- Stratify their employees in dead-end jobs
- Resist introduction of improved methods and equipment
- Rely too much on outside consulting services—or conversely, reject such help even when it is needed.

Not all departments, of course, exhibit these human failings. But given a company with many, too many, departments, all under pressure, some of them will. The treatment of choice is O.D. intervention. Perhaps management should consider it now before things get worse. Perhaps again, it has departmentalized too much and too soon.

GUERILLA WARFARE

Though not the most evident of practices, guerilla fighting among departments occurs in some—by no means all—organizations. Departments come to "have it in" for each other. They develop a great internal loyalty. With it they also may develop an external hostility. A few examples: the quality control people see themselves as referees calling penalties on the production people, rather than as coaches and trainers. The operating departments foster antipathies and rivalries with staff departments ("$85,000 to install that extruder? Get those engineers out of my hair and I'll do it for ten!"). Sales people ridicule marketing's efforts ("All that money for commercials that don't even name the product till the last frame!"). Brand managers scorn sales people as mere order writers ("Couldn't even handle our building-suppliers promo! That's why it flopped!").

Not content with sniping over the borders, departments sometimes try to steal one another's responsibilities. Department heads take to dealing directly with outside suppliers rather than go through Purchasing. The finishing department smuggles a mechanic on to its payroll so it won't have to beg Maintenance for repairs. Market Research quietly engages an outside service bureau for computer work because it never gets a high priority from the central computer department.

On a larger scale they even steal business from each other. "Some of the toughest competition First Bank System Inc. used to face was among its own units. Until recently, its Minneapolis and St. Paul banks relished undercutting each other to win a customer. Now Mr. Dixon has halted that intramural rivalry, putting the two big institutions under the same management team. It is part of a series of consolidation moves throughout the empire that are aimed at cutting costs and increasing efficiency."[1]

All these are department phenomena. They are not the little person-to-person feuds that we all know and that the personnel counsellor tries to deal with. They are bigger, they come to seem natural, they are even fun. And they hurt the organization, for they substitute internal jousting for assault against external competitors. When departments are at odds, the company suffers. But does anyone know or care about these little wars? Guide rule: Attention to energy-wasting feuds created by departmentalization releases more energy for fighting the company's battle.

ETC.

I do not mean to suggest that departments are the great hidden evil of corporate life, but they do create their own problems. In addition to those I have mentioned others are:

- They encourage territoriality.
- Without careful control they lead to unequal treatment of employees; some are overgenerous in personal appraisals and merit increases, others stingy.
- They encourage resistance to transfer and promotion of good employees.
- They channel employees into rigid, sometimes dead-end, promotional ladders.
- They have their own life cycles and tend to resist extinction when the real need for them has passed.
- Their duties themselves can make them, if things get out of hand, natural enemies. Sales versus Credit Administration for example; one wants every possible customer, the other only the reasonably solvent ones.

- They can impose on others rules, forms, and procedures that become paramount to the service or function for which they exist. For example, the requirement of complicated, multicopy work orders for piffling jobs.
- They tend to structure into internal levels, departments within departments. The result is a band of high-priced intermediate "supervisors" who are essentially message-passers and coordinator-administrators.

All these problems and those I have previously described are part of the price of largeness and the departmentalization that it entails. They lie under cover in the organization chart, being dealt with only when one or another of them becomes unbearably disruptive. Some companies never experience them. Some companies do, but in a way that is unperceived by upper-level executives. For those that do, reorganization may help to break up destructive internecine practices. But even this may not work, and in that case the answer is Abby's: See a counselor—in this case, a professional consulting organizational psychologist.

CHESSING IT

As with the pieces on a chessboard, whose potency and utility depend heavily on where they are placed with relation to others, so with departments. Anyone scrutinizing departments' effectiveness should ask: Are they in the best place in the organization to accomplish their purposes?

What their place should be depends on what is expected of them. And this may be different today from what it was when they were last assigned. For example, consider branch warehouses. While the firm is expanding its customer lists and its sales corps, Sales may be too concentrated on growth to give effective management to warehouses as well. For this reason the latter may have been placed under, say, Operations. But later when the market has stabilized, physical warehousing may be transferred to Sales to permit control sensitively geared to customer service. Similarly, Price Administration may be part of Marketing under some circumstances; part of Accounting, next to its sister Accounts Receivable, under others. In some companies Quality Control is subsumed under Operations to emphasize manufacturing's ultimate accountability for quality, to which the control department contributes. In others it is wholly separate, perhaps a division of its own, to provide a system of objective checks and balances. Guide rule: Place departments where they can do the most good under contemporary conditions.

Departmental placing may also solve problems. For example, the machine shop complains that the in-house foundry is not cleaning castings properly, resulting in broken tools and more machining time. "Why, they're leaving stumps of gates and risers on every valve body!" Answer: transfer casting finishing from foundry to machine shop supervision. No more complaints, on that subject at least. Guide rule: Reassignment of functions may sometimes solve interdepartmental complaints.

Departmental placing need not be a matter of natural blend. Some functions, as a matter of security, should never be parts of others. Accounts Payable does not belong in the purchasing department despite—because of—their community of interest. Nor does Payroll belong in Personnel or Accounts Receivable in Sales. Guide rule: Auditor's requirements must be considered in placing departments, even if seemingly at the expense of efficiency.

Certain functions may be departmentalized or not depending on their size. For example, if the sheet metal shop consists of only three or four people it may be combined administratively with the carpentry shop. Consisting of fifty people, it might well be an entity in itself. Guide rule: Specialization of function should not alone dictate departmentalizing.

Departmental placement is a tricky subject. Departments should not be moved about willy-nilly just because someone has loaded the boss's ears with complaints and promises at lunchtime. At the same time where they are put does affect their performance and hence, that of the company. The organization in a changing company need not be fixed for all time like the squares on a chessboard; it should be changing and adaptive, like the deployment of the pieces in the game.

HOW TO DO IT

Baffled executives basically unfamiliar with their companies sometimes try to reduce overhead by mandating across-the-board cutbacks. "Reduce the number of employees in every department by 10 percent!" This is like running the lawnmower over the flower bed to get rid of the weeds. And it is unfair to both the employees and the company. For a more selective, less damaging, and ultimately more profitable approach they might look to departmental weeding. But how? Here are some steps:

1. Prepare a list of departments (using the term in its broadest sense). Usually this is equivalent to a list of managerial and supervisory titles. Accompany it with a brief description of the end results that each is accountable for.

2. Ask if these end results could be met by an outside supplier. Often *when all charges are taken into account* competitive outsiders can provide the

service at no more cash cost. Additionally, they may offer more schedule flexibility and more "with-it" facilities. And getting rid of fixed departmental expenses lowers the breakeven point.

3. Look for departments whose end results are not needed at all. This does not mean focusing on easy targets like human relations, that perennial patsy, whose services are probably most essential when the company is in a state of organizational earthquake. It does mean looking at those departments so insulated in jargon and technologies that no one is sure just what they do. Perhaps they should be trimmed out, perhaps not; but they should be examined. Look for relay stations—organizational levels whose incumbents merely pass information, requests, and approvals between those above and those below, never making a live-or-die decision on their own. Are there commissar agencies whose only purpose is second-guessing the troops, as in Buck Gray's company? Are there any departments still performing work long since taken over by the computer? Are there departments doing the marketing—sans budget for advertising, promotion, and research—for product lines that have shrunk to insignificance? Any that once provided coordinating services for branch offices, factories, or warehouses that have now been consolidated? Why not clean out the attic? Put the employees of these departments where they will be doing something useful.

4. Examine the number of employees per supervisor in each department. If it is low, consider how to raise it by merging several of these small departments under one supervisor. Perhaps there are groups of jobs, now nominally supervised, that are so self-governing that they need little more than routine administrative management. Three programmers, for example, or four factory nurses, need not be distinguished as an organizational entity with a full-time supervisor.

5. Determine if spans of control and attention are too narrow. Here everything depends on circumstances. Management of a variety of different things requires a narrow span; of similar things, a wide one. For example, one person probably can not adequately supervise forty draftspersons all working on different projects—not, at least, without intermediate supervision. On the other hand, one person might well be the sole district manager of forty auto parts stores. A broader span means fewer supervisors.

6. Determine if various departments mesh properly. Are there duplications, as in the inventory records previously mentioned? Are there overlaps between central office and branch staffs, with the result that each unduly takes up the other's time, in effect working twice on every job?

7. Ask if dispersed functions would in some cases actually be more effective than massed ones. For example, a company having several divisions or branches may find that a small drafting department in each is more productive than a single centralized one. Specialization speeds up the work, and there are fewer problems of priority, scheduling, and communicating. A similar approach can be taken to other activities: ac-

counting, plant engineering, quality control, and even marketing. The trick is to insert the smaller, decentralized groups into existing organizations without creating ten new department heads for every superseded one.

8. Check if certain departments, if physically adjacent, could share records, equipment, or clerical help. In the same vein, can geographically separate departments be combined into one location with attendant savings. For example, a western bank chain consolidated all its consumer-loan makers, formerly scattered among branches, into a central location. Other firms have consolidated sales branches, warehouses, and factories. But such agglomerations must be handled with caution, for overcentralizing has its dangers too: less flexibility, poorer customer relations, increased union susceptibility. Even a jump in freight or utility rates may gobble up expected savings.

9. Are there instances where a plethora of departments slows the company down? For example, can nothing be done quickly because everything must be multiply reviewed and approved—the problem that Hisao Tsubouchi dealt with so drastically?

10. Not everything can be learned from a study of the charts. People who work in the organization know it best, and what they have to say is worth listening to. Interdepartmental squabbles, jealousies, and frustrations are clues to simplification opportunities. For example, here is a department head who has hatched a scheme for folding someone else's department into his or her own, clearly a transparent attempt to get a higher salary evaluation. And yet, if the transfer can shuck off middle-management positions and interdepartmental boundaries, it may be just what the company needs.

11. Merely relocating a department may be a "consciousness-raising" act that pays off in performance. For example, consider a product research department that reports in the operations division. Transferring it to the marketing division takes its members from the manufacturing orientation in which they have learned to live and exposes them to a customer-sensitive ambiance that may enhance their overall value. Departmental placement can affect departmental results.

12. Finally, to prevent future recurrence of the departmental problem, a simple and inviolable rule: Since a new department can, in a few years, cost as much as a major piece of equipment, no new department may be instituted, nor new supervisory position created, without a formal request similar to an appropriation request (supported with payoffs), being submitted to the president. The wise president postpones decision on all such requests received.

CONCLUSION

For the cost-bitten organization mass divestment of employees may seem the only answer. But it is a primitive one and may leave the company crippled and still struggling. Far more effective and perhaps humane is a selective adjustment of departmental responsibilities and structure. While this too may result in disemployment, it does so without personal finger-pointing and implied guilt. It has the additional merit of getting at the primary cause of cost proliferation: the departmental hotbeds in which positions multiply. The benefits are two-fold: expense reduction and organization agility. For in both the large and the small company, departments can paradoxically cause more tie-ups than the people they shelter.

Accordingly, a thorough understanding of the contribution and cost of departments is essential background information for contemplated reorganization.

NOTE

1. *Wall Street Journal*, 26 July 1985.

9

Groundwork

A well-planned reorganization comprises several steps, some of which have now been described:

1. The Initiators have outlined the nature of the change to be made.
2. They have stated its objectives.
3. They have assigned the administration of the reorganization to a person or group.
4. Policies have been enunciated governing the reorganization.
5. Comprehensive background information has been obtained to guide the specific changes.

CHARTS

At this point the Planner sharpens pencils and spreads paper on the drawing board. It is time to rough out a new organization chart. This chart embodies not only all the changes that the Planner has received from the Initiators but also others that have been suggested in interviews. At its top it may be fairly firm; there is no question, for example, that the president wants to split the marketing and sales division into two separate entities. And as it progresses downward the Planner may have a good fix on certain specific changes: the elimination of certain departments, for example, that can be replaced by outside suppliers. Also, the Planner knows if the Initiators have narrowed in on particular individuals for removal; and additionally there is the list of people who are apt to take early retirement; so that blank spots and possible replacements, if any, can be shown. The chart begins to take shape.

Its further elaboration may include additional factors that have come to light since the original assignment. For example:

- Examination of the existing charts has suggested structural defects—say, the presence of multiple and unnecessary levels of supervision—that might just as well be corrected now.

- Certain departments have turned out to be excess baggage. Why should they be exempt from general housecleaning?

- The originally proposed changes rebound on other parts of the organization. For example, consolidating six factories into three unexpectedly lessens the workload in the physical distribution department. Or absorption of an acquired company's management into the headquarters office entails expanding the crew of systems analysts. Or elimination of coupon redemption means fewer clerks in the mailroom.

- From interviews have come suggestions for profitable realignment going beyond those originally contemplated. ("Instead of trying to restructure the raw materials inventory control section, why don't you just merge it into Purchasing?")

Though the chart is in effect a rough draft, it should embody all practicable ideas that have been suggested to equip the company for improved performance.

Lining up the new and old charts, the Planner compares the changes with the original objectives. Has what was wanted been accomplished? Have additional, unforeseen opportunities applied for recognition?

At this point the chart may still not be complete. The Planner simply does not know how to handle the blocks and people in its profuse lower sections. And there is not time to negotiate changes individually with each supervisor. It might be better to convene a meeting of all those managers concerned and let them solve problems jointly. In this reorganization there may have to be some horse trading. And there will also be some of the reluctance that accompanies any transition and a tendency to resist proposed cuts in the staffing of one's own area. All this can best be dealt with in a group get-together where the managers involved say who and what go where. There will be a sense of shared commitment and of mutual contribution to the objectives of the enterprise at hand. When the meeting is successfully concluded, the chart of the new organization will have been filled out in its entirety. It will be derived from the knowledge of those most familiar with its parts and supported by the consensus of those who will have to make the reorganization meet its objectives. We will have more to say about this meeting.

HEAD COUNT

Chart comparison should be accompanied by an estimated head count, before and after. The Initiators need facts. If one of the objectives was a reduction in personnel, evidence must certify that it will be achieved.

Not all reorganizations, of course, are pull-backs. For example, when an acquisition is being blended in, a new headquarters chart may show more people than the old one (though probably not more than the combined old ones). And a reorganization for growth may well carry more people on the new chart than on the old one. The transformation is aimed at making money, not saving it.

But if a force reduction is in fact called for, the new chart must reflect this diminution. Whether the objective was expressed in absolute numbers of departures or in a percentage cut of the payroll, the Planner must determine its total and then subtract from that the removals represented on the chart so far. What is left must be assigned on a reasonable basis to the remaining unfilled-in portions of the chart.

With this assignment the overall before and after head count can be broken down into departmental before and after counts. How these are to be achieved is one of the things to be thrashed out, not without some anguish, in the meeting we have spoken of.

How do you know what the ultimate number of employees should be? One way is to have the controller estimate how much the overhead should amount to in order to meet a desired selling price/profit level. This can then be translated into an equivalent number of people. Unless this objective can be reached, the company will not attain its financial objectives.

It may be mentioned, incidentally, that determining how many people are in the company is not always an easy thing to do with utter accuracy. You cannot just have the computer count the pay checks it is printing. Some of these are for the two-weeks notice pay or salary continuation of people who have recently been let go; some are for advances ahead of vacation; some for paid leave of absence; and there may be people who, though employees, are on temporary layoff, not getting a check at all, as well as people just hired who will not get a check until next time around. There may even be checks for part-time workers—do they count or not? How about temporary employees? Some of them are handling surges in the workload, some filling in for absent regular employees. They are certainly a drain on the cash but may not show up on the payroll check register—should they be included?

Instead of counting checks, you might just count names on the personnel roster. Of course not all these "names" are actually working at any one time, or even, for that matter, getting paid. Some are on layoff. Some are absent for jury duty, illness, vacation, death or illness in the family, or pregnancy. Then there is the matter of seasonality. Are you totalling the employees at peak season or at the ebb—or on the average? Business fluctuation accounts for differences: the number of employees at work in many factories and mail-order houses, for example, swings up and down with the volume of sales.

Instead of dealing with the number of people, it might be thought that the right number to use is budgeted positions. But, as Buck Gray knew, some budgeted positions are only padding for safety, held in place to ensure an ability to run within the budget. Cutting them back may or may not be a real savings.

A stipulated percentage cut is also worth thinking about. It may seem like a fair and objective way of expecting the same relative sacrifice from all areas. But is it? Here is a department full of telephone solicitors. Take away, say, 20 percent of them, and it will still function with no trouble (though with possible adverse effects on future sales). Here is a computer hardware department, under a boss that has it as tightly staffed as a submarine. A 20 percent cut may be catastrophic.

All these uncertainties mean only that the Planner must be sure that the Initiators demanding a personnel reduction are specific in what they are referring to and understand its implications. Equally the Planner must see that all reductions claimed by managers and supervisors are measured on the same scale.

FINANCIAL ESTIMATE

The preliminary proposal also includes an estimate of the costs and savings of the change. These fall into several categories. There is first a comparison of the payroll (including fringes) before and after. To this is added those overhead expenses that vary directly with the presence of the employees involved: telephone, travel, "perks," subscriptions and memberships, supplies, space rental, utilities, insurance, and taxes.

Second, there are the one-time personnel expenses of the change itself. For a reduction in personnel these include severance pay, accrued vacation and holiday pay, annuities, "buyouts," outplacement service fees, relocation expenses, resumé assistance, special job-hunting arrangements, perhaps even legal fees. On a growth chart a different set of one-time expenses enter in: search and employment fees, relocation expenses, and new facilities for the added positions in factory, laboratory, or office.

Third, when relocation of facilities is part of the reorganization plan, continuing change will run all through the expense ledger: taxes, insurance, fuels, utilities, rentals, freight-in and freight-out, maintenance materials, depreciation if there are allied changes in facilities—the length of the list depends on the circumstances.

Fourth, the final proposal should also include firmer estimates of the cash flows accompanying the shutdown or transfer of facilities. Into this category fall mothballing, maintenance and protection, relocation, possibly writeoff, possibly resale. Conversely, in an expansion reorganization, the cost of additional facilities, either on- or off-site, must be approximated. In some cases other related expenses can crop up. For example, if the reorganization includes an abandonment of certain product lines, inventory disposal may incur some one-shot losses.

One-time expense may also occur in a business merger. In some mergers or acquisitions the participating companies are allowed to continue as entities, completely decentralized and united only in reporting to the top. In other situations, (e.g. rearranging to have one organization take the place of two or to have one of them introduce its expertise into the other) additional outlays may be necessary. For example, with General Motors' acquisition of Electronic Data Systems, experts from the latter were assigned to integrate all the separate and different data processing systems in the GM divisions, something like that mad king who tried to make a roomful of clocks tick in unison; the cost of this endeavor seems to be one associated more with organizing than with simply buying another company.

Fifth, there may be upcoming investments that the reorganization will obviate. For example, Factory A may have a new waste disposal plant in its capital budget for next year; but if it is shut down this outlay will not be necessary. Items of this sort are not exactly savings, since the money has not yet been spent. But they do help in reaching a decision on financial aspects: if you spend money now on reorganizing, you will not have to spend it next year on the waste plant. Sometimes it is legitimate to look at impending expenses in a similar manner. For example, absorption of some of the staff of an acquired company may require renting more office space, and this potential new expense can be avoided by rationalizing the payroll now.

With the proposal still in its formative stages all these estimates need be only rough indices of the financial aspects of the change. But they are useful. They can, for one thing, suggest whether the change so far outlined is close to meeting any long- and short-range financial criteria posed by the original objectives. If not, either the objectives or the plan must be reapproached. Second, they come into play as part of the comparison of merits of alternative plans. Third, they may affect the timing of the reorganization; with a heavy ingoing dollar load, it may be desirable to phase the reorganization over two fiscal years.

CHANGE LISTS

As an aid to those who review the proposal, brief lists of major changes may be prepared (see Figure 9.1). These barebones lists are intended only for informative purposes to assist those reviewing the charts. They may, indeed, lead to revisions. ("I'm not sure Kelly is really qualified for that Organization Development job. Maybe we ought to look outside.") After a final proposal has been approved they will, suitably revamped, be expanded for use in the implementation planning stage.

If alternative organization charts are to be presented for selection, then matching alternative change lists must accompany them.

In these lists newly created positions may occur. What do they accomplish? Understanding of both the charts and the lists is assisted with a glossary of new position titles and brief descriptions (see Figure 9.2).

PRELIMINARY PRESENTATION

With materials in hand, the Planner is ready for a preliminary presentation to the Initiators of the reorganization. These props consist of a reminder statement of the original objectives, the old and the new organization charts, the lists of changed jobs and personnel, head counts, and the cost/savings estimate.

Such a presentation is preferably made in a meeting, with accompanying flip charts, wall posters, and slides. Handouts—folders containing the same material—may also be provided. The small audience may make notes in these folders, and if necessary, take them home overnight for further study (with appropriate reminders of confidentiality).

Then in this or the next day's session, further changes or modifications are suggested, debated, and rejected or accepted. Alternatives, if included, are sorted out for a decision on the most workable. At the meeting's end the proposal may be quite different from the opening version. Seeing the first sketchy objectives now fleshed out in potential reality has a sobering effect. Perhaps these rosy objectives now appear impossible to attain. Perhaps the cost of change is higher or the savings lower than expected. Strengthening some parts of the organization turns out to weaken others. Talking about the change

POSITION LIST

Position Title	Now Reports To	Will Report To
VP Administration (new)	--	President
VP Communications	President	VP Administration (new)
VP Personnel	President	VP Administration (new)
Mgr. Cons. Rel.	G. M. Sales	VP Communications
	etc.	

PEOPLE LIST

Name	Present Position	New Position
L. Reed	VP Personnel	VP Administration
N. Bell	G. M. Org. Dev.	VP Personnel
H. Kelly	Mgr. Employment	G. M. Org. Dev.
J. Wood	Interviewer	Mgr. Employment
M. Bailey	VP Advertising	(Unpositioned)
	etc.	

Figure 9.1

may uncover adverse effects on customer service, on key employees, on outside observers, even on cash flow.

More optimistically, the proposal may open up new vistas of improvement never dreamed of at the start. This means more revision.

Thus, the preliminary proposal is adjusted, either on the spot or in a complete remodeling and resubmission. When finally approved,

<u>NEW POSITIONS</u>

<u>Position Title</u>	<u>Description</u>
Manager, Security	Directly responsible for security at headquarters offices. Indirectly consults on and supervises security at all branches.
Manager, Market Research	Manages newly-created market research department, unifying research activities formerly spread among product managers.
Manager, Distribution	Replaces three eliminated positions: Manager, Traffic; Manager, Fleet; Manager, Warehousing.

etc.

Figure 9.2

still on the basis of approximations, it is ready for conversion to a final proposal.

REFINING

Between the preliminary and final proposals lies a wealth of detail that must now be worked through.

First, the proposed organization chart must be put in its next-to-last form (further changes may be expected when final approval is agreed on). This means that all blocks must be connected in their most effective relationships. Position titles must be filled in and employee names entered in all possible levels. Much of these data will have come from background information, from the objectives statements, and from suggestions made in the preliminary presentation. Along with finalization of the organization chart comes an update of the lists of position changes and people changes.

Ideally this is done in conjunction with the managers involved, who are most knowledgeable on the subject matter. As sections of the final chart are filled in, for example, the Planner consults with persons familiar with the assignment to get new ideas and to correct awkward configurations. In some cases only a few people at the top may be accessible. In others, depending on the company climate, the degree of threat latent in the change, and the company's policy on confidentiality, lower-level supervisors and even bottom-of-the-chart hourly employees, may participate. The planning is most rewardingly carried out when nourished by the knowledge and judgment of those who will have to make the newly-shaped organization work. These are the employees who will occupy the new arrangement. They know what combinations will jibe and what won't. They know what physical moves are feasible. ("Well, yeah, you can move that lab. But it'll cost. Some of their instruments sit on foundations going down to bedrock.") They know which subordinates will best enable them to fulfill their accountabilities.

The more consultation, the more good ideas—and of equal importance—the more ownership in the change and the greater its acceptability. This acceptability is no small asset. It makes the difference between a post-change atmosphere of disheartened resentment and one of energized revivification.

It is not always possible to enlist full participation. The sensitivity of the conversion affects freedom of discussion and this in turn goes back to the policy on confidentiality. The Planner may be able to work only with the core group who participated in earlier planning.

Secondly, the Planner must now reduce the preliminary financial estimates to final form. For arriving at the costs and savings of exits, representatives of the personnel and accounting departments may be enlisted. With their help the expense flow associated with immediate separation costs and the future cash flow associated with changes in payroll and overhead can be derived from the specific moves contemplated. A similar approach applies to any new hires scheduled for the future organization. Income and balance sheet changes related to facilities alterations may call for inputs from the accounting and engineering departments as a firm basis for the final proposal.

PROPOSAL

With all the blocks and numbers firmly placed, the presentation for preliminary approval occurs. In a meeting, attended by Initiators of the project, collegial members of the executive group, and perhaps outside management consultants, the data are reviewed. A checklist displays the specific steps that meet the original objectives, plus any added features that, having emerged in the investigation, will fit in advantageously.

If an approval is given to proceed, the discussion now turns to the real-world steps of implementation, which are discussed in Chapter 10.

10

Transition Onset

Between the final decision on what the revised organization shall consist of and the actual realization of this objective lies a period of metamorphosis from old to new. During this transition the organization is, like a butterfly getting its wings unfolded after creeping out of its cocoon, in a vulnerable position. The period is a sensitive one both for the company's business interests and its employees' personal ones.

If you are in charge of it you want it to be quick, clear, and effective. Presumably something was a problem and you count on the reorganization to correct it. You certainly do not want the transition to create new problems. While it occurs, phones and mail still have to be answered, orders recorded and transmitted, bills paid and receipts deposited, materials received and shipments sent out, and the quality of the product maintained. Major design, construction, marketing, and programming projects must not grind to a halt. Customers and suppliers must not encounter a spongy mass of "I don't know who's in charge of that now." Do it right and the company will emerge, like the butterfly, in splendid shape.

If you are an employee, caught up in the change, your interest in the transition is a little different. Of course you hope that the company (assuming you are still with it) will be better off. After all, it is your livelihood. You hope, too, that some of the internal job problems you have been coping with will be cleared up. Beyond this there is your own welfare. Whatever is going to happen, you want it to be got over with so you know where you stand. Are you getting a new assignment that will brighten your career path? Are you getting an opportunity to capitalize on the talents you know you have, even to work on the very job you find most fascinating? Are you getting a raise?

Or is your lot going to be worse? Yanked off the project they told you was so important? Demoted (with or without a pay cut)? Passed over, stranded? Publicly shamed? Or worst: fired?

Or perhaps the transition is scary. Transferred to the meanest boss in the company. Put on a job you're not sure you can handle. Separated from your former supportive fellow workers. Shifted to the most dismal office or noisiest shop. Stuck, if you're a boss, with having to fire members of your departmental clan.

Both to get at the rewards it promises and to minimize the disruption it causes, the transition should be no more than a brief incident in the life of the company. This means it must be carefully thought out.

Generally speaking it consists of several stages:

1. Deciding on timing.
2. Notifying upper-level managers.
3. Working out unresolved details.
4. Notifying the rest of those affected.
5. Following up on things still left hanging.

TIMING

Often two decisions must be made on timing. One concerns phasing, the other the actual calendar date of change. Both depend on individual company circumstances.

Phasing occurs when it is decided to break the reorganization into diachronous sections. For example, in the case of an organizational contraction, it may be that certain factories are to be merged and only later are the warehouses holding their output to be combined. The conversion from company salesmen to sales reps or brokers may be done step-by-step, one region at a time. Mill A may be closed; but not until Mill B has absorbed its production will the closing of Mill C be scheduled. The company can handle the integration of subsidiary M with its own operations but only when this has been completed can it tackle integration of subsidiary N. A cutback of headquarters staff may pave the way for corresponding reductions at outlying branches.

Projected expansion, on the other hand, presents other options. Starting and staffing a new factory, for example, will not occur until product sales have reached a predetermined level. A change from functional to product orientation will be made now but a further conversion to subsidiary companies later as the businesses grow.

Quality Control, now an independent function, will be put into Operations now, and then eight months later when it is in place, Research will move into Operations also, thus enlarging that division's scope and control.

Wherever there is a Phase I, it is worked out in detail for the first transition. Subsequent phases are projected in the rough, their implementation to be refined as they fall due.

A decision on phasing may come early on, and as we mentioned in Chapter 3, is a possible element of policy. On the other hand, the need for phasing may not appear until the planning of the actual reorganization shows that smooth transition makes it essential.

A second decision is: When will the most immediate transition take place? This too depends on the circumstances. If it is a relatively easy one—say, absorbing Data Systems into the controller's department—the answer may be "right away!" More complex ones, however, may require special planning on the calendar, with consideration for both business continuity and human relations.

The business itself may make certain dates more or less opportune than others. Looking at some of them in an "all other things being equal" view:

- If formulation of the budget is a major annual undertaking, then a transition coming just before it, rather than just after, will hold budget revisions to a minimum.
- If reconstruction of the strategic business plan is a major annual event, a reorganization coming just after it rather than just before it can adapt to its provisions.
- If there is an annual shipping peak, changes affecting the physical distribution operations can most readily be handled after it is over.
- If a major promotional or sales drive is imminent, a sweeping reorganization in Marketing or Sales may interfere with its prosecution and should if possible be deferred.
- If the business is seasonal, a reorganization just after rather than on the eve of the crest may create less disruption. You do not reorganize a university one week before registration.
- If it turns out that the company is in danger of becoming someone else's acquisition, the reorganization may just as well be postponed till the dust settles.
- If the company is engaged in a lawsuit requiring access to witnesses and files, the bearing of a reorganization on the testimony in support of its case should be considered.
- If the company is in the midst of union negotiations, reorganization affecting members may have a favorable or adverse influence, and its timing should be taken into account in this regard.
- If there is an independently planned change in the top executive ranks—say, the replacement of a vice president with an outsider, reorganization

of that executive's area should be deferred until the new incumbent can have a hand in it.

- If the company follows a practice of giving periodic salary and wage adjustment *en masse*, reorganization timing should keep this in mind. ("On the first of the month they gave me a raise. On the eighth, they demoted me and cut my salary. What a way to run a company!")
- If a large number of employees are going to be on vacation, reorganization at that time will encounter difficulties of notification.
- If the costs or savings of the change are expected to be large, the company may wish to consider which fiscal year they are to fall in.

As for the employees, reorganization is bound to be elative to some, wounding to others, and for simple humanity (or less sentimentally, good morale) it should be timed with them in mind. Some parts of the year just do not seem attractive when job losses are in the works. Right before Christmas, for example. Or just after it, for that matter, when bills must be paid. Just before vacation—a good or bad time?

Even the day of the week matters. A shake-up on Friday or before a holiday weekend leaves everyone stewing for the next few days and exchanging misinformation on the telephone. Monday starts right off with a high sphygmomanometer reading. Any other day is better. It makes the very next morning available for questions and for getting on with the transition while its momentum is high, without an intervening dead spell.

Taking all the "if's" into account, there may be very few windows in the year that are ideal for switching things around. The reorganization may have to compete with other activities for time which provides the reason to make it go like clockwork.

INTERWEAVING

The starting gun goes off when people are notified of the change. Notification is the first step in transition. And planning it rasies questions:

- Who in the company is going to be notified?
- In what sequence?
- By whom?
- What are they going to be told?

As a side, but not unimportant task, notification may also be required for persons external to the organization (which we will come to).

It might seem that the notification process is so straightforward as to need no comment. The president tells the vice presidents about the change (if they do not already know), the vice presidents tell their general managers, the general managers tell the supervisors and so on down the line until the subleader of groundskeepers tells the trash-dumper that he has been promoted to lawnmower operator. But nothing is that simple.

The problem is that no one can identify in the preliminary stages every possible move; let alone name which particular employees, if any, are to be released. It may be clear that the vice president of research and quality control is about to retire without replacement, his area being split between Operations and Engineering. But how split? Neither the Planner nor the respective VP's of Operations and Engineering may have hands-on knowledge of every compartment in the research and quality control division. For example, here is the metallurgy lab: it is running several research projects and it also performs quality control tests on incoming metals; and some of its employees work on both. Should it be sundered and if so, who goes where? Or should it be assigned as a whole to one division, selling its services to the other, an arrangement that at once introduces day-to-day conflicts of priority? Knowledgeable people are going to have to answer these questions before the lab employees can be told whom they will be working for.

Limited reorganizations do not encounter this type of problem. If the dean of the drama school, for example, intends to replace a couple of instructors and combine lighting and set design under one head and bring in a voice coach from the music department, the dean's empire is small enough that the whole thing can quickly be laid out.

Consider, by contrast, a really extensive reorganization: the CEO of a 50,000 employee company wants to reduce the number of people reporting to him, convert from functional to product orientation, prepare two product lines for sale to outsiders, turn as many internal departments as possible over to external suppliers, consolidate three factories, and cut the payroll by 7,000 employees, without any inter-ruption to sales or shipments. Though it may seem like trying to overhaul the engine of a 747 while in flight from New York to London, there is no reason why a change of this magnitude cannot be accom-plished fairly quickly and with full attention to the welfare of both the company and its employees. It cannot, of course, be worked out by a small planning staff. Members of the managerial ranks must participate. But in being asked to participate they must be notified of the change, which means notifying them of its effects on them personally, as well. So in planning a substantial transition, there must be an interweaving of the notification and detailing processes. Some people must be told, and then they work out the steps for telling the next group of people.

Obviously those who are in on the change from the start do not need to be told about what is up. They originated it. But there may be others at their level—we will assume that it is the first level under the CEO—who are not privy to it. So for starters, the CEO has to tell them. He may do so in various ways.

For example, a CEO reviewing with his secretary what he has just said to an obnoxious vice president: "So I said to him, 'Jones, I've had it up to here with you. You are fired. Get out!' " Secretary (putting hand to mouth in dismay): "Oh, you didn't!" CEO: "Well, what did you expect me to do? Curtsy to him?" (This is after the CEO has lain awake for three nights rehearsing speeches that he never used.)

In a more rational scene the CEO might tell the vice president that:

1. As they both know, things haven't worked out as they might have wished.
2. Regardless of why, the vice president can realize his or her potential more fully in another environment.
3. His or her tenure with the company is being terminated immediately.
4. A specialist in outplacement services is waiting in the next room to discuss the specifics of the departure arrangements, which are very favorable.
5. The CEO wishes to say personally that he wishes all good luck, hopes to retain a personal bond, will do all possible to help, etc. (there being always the possibility that the CEO will someday need a favor from the exiting vice president).

In another form of high-level change, the CEO tells the vice president, who probably has a strong inkling of what is coming, that:

1. The company is being reorganized in order to....
2. As part of this reorganization the vice president will be assuming additional accountabilities, for which he or she has already demonstrated great qualifications.
3. In its new form the organization will look like this....
4. The vice president is asked to inform the general managers reporting to him or her of the changes, preparatory to a meeting in which further details will be worked out.

To assist in telling immediate subordinates of the reorganization, the vice president is given a "talk-memo," which we will come to a little later. With its help he or she passes the word to the next group of key managers who are to be informed. All this should not take more than a day.

In this way notification at an upper level precedes participation in planning the transformation at lower levels. There is an interweaving of telling and doing. First you tell key people. Then you enlist their help in shaping what goes on further down, which they presently will be telling to those affected.

GET-TOGETHER

This blend of informing followed by further planning is something like putting stones in place to cross a stream. You place a stone, then reach from it to place the next stone.

In a large reorganization a cadre of upper-level managers are individually informed of the change; then they are brought together for a joint analysis of what comes next.

This group contribution demands hard decisions, giving and taking and trading off, relinquishing as well as assuming responsibilities, and keeping the big picture in mind while filling in the specifics. It is best performed in a meeting at an off-site location, free from interruption. If it has been adequately prepared for, it should not require more than one or two days. When it is complete the transition is ready to go into high gear.

Who attends this meeting?—those who fully control the reorganization at hand.

If the change is company-wide, the president or CEO should start the session off with an introductory, explanatory talk emphasizing the purposes of the reorganization. If it concerns only a division, a subsidiary, or a branch (such as a factory or sales area) it can be led by the person in charge of that unit.

Meetings can be cascaded. For example, a small group of headquarters executives and managers might devise changes in the headquarters staff and the heads of its major external units (such as the aforementioned branch factories and offices). Then each of these subunits would conduct internal reorganization meetings following guidelines issued by the Planner and the headquarters group.

In anticipation of the meeting the participants may be asked, perhaps two weeks ahead, to arrange their schedules to be in town at the chosen time, without necessarily being informed of the purpose. Then, a day or two ahead of the conference, they are individually informed of the overall nature of the change, of its effect on them personally, and of the need to finalize its ramifications.

They meet. They work out what is to be done. They arrive at a schedule for next steps. But what are they to work with? The Planner must see that all necessary information bearing on the change is readily available to facilitate speedy and valid decisions by those convening.

Foremost in such information, if the reorganization is an "economy" one, is a statement of how many employees are to be released. Presumably this is a given, and not subject to relaxation. The statement must be broken down into categories: the number of releases that automatically flow from elimination of departments, the number that will be accounted for by early retirements, and the number that remain to be identified by those present, at least preliminarily allocated to departments. In addition, for use in the meeting, there should be:

1. A wall poster listing the objectives.

2. A wall poster, block form, portraying the prechange organization.

3. Another poster displaying the proposed new organization. This one may be incomplete, requiring further entries, especially in the lower floors of the organizational structure, which is one of the things this meeting is to accomplish. The group has to recommend where blocks are to be positioned and put names in them.

4. A file of personal appraisals. Though the contents may not be 100 percent reliable, since they perhaps include opinions of supervisors who are being released for their very inability to handle people, they may be of some assistance in deciding who goes where, who stays, and who leaves.

5. The previously described position list, which will now be expanded to show new positions, transfers, combinations, and deletions decided on in the meeting.

6. The aforementioned people list. This list, previously sketchy, is now greatly expanded. It is going to be used not only for the discussion at hand but for the follow-up activation of the plans. A sample is shown in Figure 10.1. In this sample the new status of L. Murphy, E. Rodriguez, and F. Edwards is spelled out. It was arrived at in the first round of planning, before the meeting now occurring. Why are not the new statuses of S. Morris and M. Cook also identified? Because it is not yet known if these people are to be retained in the purchasing department. Opportunities for transferring them elsewhere, however, may turn up in the discussions attending the large meeting. If they remain in Purchasing or a new place is found for them, it will be entered in the "To" column. If not, the "To" column will be marked "Released." Thus, the future status of every employee is accounted for.

    On this list the column headed "Evaluated Points" deserves some explanation. Its purpose is to give the participants some sense of whether individuals are moving to equal or better jobs. If the company has a job grade system, then the column would be headed "Job Grade." For new positions not yet evaluated or graded, the column must of course be left blank for the present.

7. Copies of the reorganization policies, as a guide to participants in the meeting.

Figure 10.1

PEOPLE LIST

Name	Payroll No.	Yrs. Svce.	Age	Position	From					To			
					Location	Dept.	Spvsr.	Eval. Pts.	Position	Location	Dept.	Spvsr.	Eval. Pts.
L. Murphy	10612	2	43	V.P.	N.Y.	PCHSG.	JBC	1170	RELEASED	–	–	–	–
E. Rodriguez	9742	20	45	Buyer	N.Y.	PCHSG.	LM	840	V.P.	N.Y.	PCHSG.	KCM	1170
F. Edwards	2897	35	55	Buyer	S.F.	PCHSG.	LM	840	RETIRED	–	–	–	–
S. Morris	11725	3	29	Asst. Buyer	N.Y.	PCHSG.	F.G.	680					
M. Cook	12421	3	30	Asst. Buyer	S.F.	PCHSG.	F.E.	680					

8. Plot plans of offices or factories if the reorganization involves physical moves that must be evaluated.

In addition there may be supporting facilities. For example, when a candidate is being considered for a position it is helpful to have a computer terminal to call up his or her educational background and previous jobs. A computer may also be employed to get changes in position and people lists quickly on to a revised chart.

Supporting staff may also be on hand; perhaps a consultant, almost certainly someone from Personnel, who will have to handle a number of chores after the meeting is over. A stenographer is useful to record salient points of the discussion as a help in answering subsequent questions about why what was decided. One other person may be helpful: an Organization Development advisor who can detect and deal with conflicts and suggest ways to avoid the well-known "interpersonal problems" that are apt to erupt when a group of managers find themselves converging on a precipice.

This meeting, if it is directed to an overall force reduction, is no picnic for many of those sitting in it. True, some of them may be headed for promotion. But it is promotion to a position that will provide fewer people resources than the predecessor had, along with greater expectations for performance. Others may be facing a disruption of the colonies that had grown under their governance. Whatever they had planned for the future will now have to be done, if at all, with what they must regard as an inadequate number of people. Employees whom they have come to know will have to be poured out of the happy family, and they will have to do both the picking and the pouring. A growth reorganization can be inspiriting, but a retractive one is bound to have its unhappy aspects. These may direct the meeting into unproductive byways. Emotional and not wholly unrealistic protests may break out in the participants' minds:

- "How'm I going to cut fifteen people out of Coupon Redemption when there are going to be three new brand managers all dreaming up new promotions?"
- "Here's Jones marked down to be fired, and you know where he is now? In the hospital with a heart attack. I'm supposed to go to his bedside and tell him he's canned?"
- "Well, yes, we can cut down the number of people in Environmental Engineering. But you may find yourself hiring some more attorneys."
- "Okay, we demote old Biggs to make room for new blood, but how's that new blood feel when they see what happens to old blood around here?"
- "Certainly I can save eighty-five salesmen by combining territories. Only let's remember we still have the same number of customers."
- "What's this, get rid of thirteen programmers after all the trouble we had

finding them? Why not cut out thirteen of those accounting clerks that feed requests to them?"

- "Listen, Fitzallen, don't tell *me* to get rid of the power plant engineers. It's your factories that keep them busy. Why don't you do a better job of running your boilers and turbines?"

In all this emotionalism the process is running away with the results. An organization psychologist may help to keep the group oriented on its mission.

The group then settles down to allocating those people and positions not yet assigned on the chart; and to determine where and how necessary reductions will be achieved.

This groping around in the nether regions of the organization is not to be done lightly, for here is the "civil service" that keeps the company running. France, after WWII, went through many changes of leadership. But it did not go to pieces. Why? Because the civil service kept the government steadily ticking along. The same thing is true of companies. Three times did Pepperidge Farms relinquish a president and three times did it install a new one, all in the space of four years. But it was still able to put bread in the supermarkets. Lower ranks kept the company in business. And tinkering with the unsung infrastructure can be dangerous. The relatively unknown credit clerk who, having heard on the phone of an impending bankruptcy, arranges calls to stop trucks on their way to deliver goods to the failing customer, may do more for today's revenues than any executive. Firing a vice president is no great shakes; the job market is teeming with potential replacements. But booting out a credit clerk familiar with an industry's customers is risky business. The same may be said for many other "civil service" employees in the substrate. They may be doing more than anyone appreciates. Decisions to cut them out should not be too cavalier; they should be at least as cautious and knowledgeable as the selection of discards from a hand of gin, which is no careless deed.

When the meeting concludes there should be:

1. A complete revised organization chart.
2. A complete Position List.
3. A complete People List, broken down into: those who remain in place; those who move; and those who are removed.

The presiding person then reminds participants of confidentiality, outlines the next steps that will carry the plans into reality, assures assistance in carrying out those steps, and thanks everyone for their efforts.

A group of parallel, high-speed processes now begins.

11

Transition Get-Ready

Just ahead is transition itself. Everyone wants to get it over as quickly as possible. No one wants employees to hear about a half a dozen moves on Monday and then go home Friday still wondering what is going to happen to them. Managers do not want people dawdling over their desks because they are not sure whether they are going to be working at those desks any more. The sales manager does not want salespersons passing up calls thinking that for all they know they will be working a quite different set of customers next month. The whole process should slip by as smoothly and easily as a crossing of the international date line. Well, almost as smoothly.

To this end advance preparations are made. These may involve the company lawyer or labor relations specialist, the pension group, the personnel people, the office facilities manager, the public relations manager, and the security head, as well as the Planner. Most of them work directly from the people list emanating from the reorganization meeting of managers. For their use the list is broken down into three groups: a tabulation of people remaining in place; one of people moving to a different job; and one of people who will be released. It contains the names of both exempts and nonexempts, salary and hourly employees.

LAW CHECK

An immediate review should be made to verify that the departure list does not, in its totality, suggest any violation of antidiscrimination law; for example, the Age Discrimination in Employment Act or

Title VII of the 1964 Civil Rights Act. Conceivably the rush to cut and pare the organization may have let loose an unconscious yet nevertheless indefensible bias against sensitive groups. Not whether bias is really present, but whether the figures show that it seems to be present, is what counts.

Company and employee vulnerability on this score is best researched by the company labor lawyer or labor relations manager. They will require a people list of departees supplemented with race and sex identification and reason for selection (such as low seniority or unfavorable appraisal history). If they discover a disproportionate culling of protected groups they are bound to recommend revision of the list for the company's safety against suit.

Additionally they may examine job and title changes within the company. Even in the absence of evidence of wholesale violation of the law, some individual cases may deserve attention. For example, the promotions manager (a man) has moved up and has been replaced by a woman who is being called only "Coordinator of Promotions." Is this an example of sex-based discrimination? Or a black female has been passed over for promotion to "Head of Personnel Records" in favor of a white male. Is this defensible? For another example, releasing an older or minority employee who has always received merit increases, favorable appraisals, and no documented warnings and whose job is to be taken over by a person of younger age or different sex or race, can raise ticklish issues. Is there any substantive support for such a decision, just in case an objection were to be raised? Or say the employee is a suspected drug addict or alcoholic; is there recorded evidence that this is truly the case, that his or her problem interfered with job performance, and that a warning of inadequacy was given?

Even discharge lists based solely on seniority have been challenged when the youngest members were also disproportionate to older ones regarding race or gender. Though the results of such cases have leaned toward support of seniority, the risk is still latent.

But regardless of the litigation possibilities, which seem to be undergoing some modification as this is written, the company should be sure that its practices do not unintentionally violate accepted standards of fair treatment to all members of the community. Action that seems to be individually justified for individual employees may seem, taken as a whole, to display a consistent attitude toward minorities. Even a single action that is internally justified—for example, forced early retirement for an incompetent—may appear to an outside observer to be age-punitive.

If a union is involved, the law department or labor relations department will also want to review the people list to be sure that any proposed changes are in accord with the provisions of the contract. Checking that seniority has governed is of course likely to be of first importance. But attention must also be given to such matters as the dissolution of departments and how their employees are treated, to how the combination or creation of departments will bear on departmental vs. company seniority, and to provisions for notice pay, severance pay, dues check-off, and benefits continuation.

Incidentally, the list may also be reviewed just to be sure that no union steward or committeeperson, protected by the contract, has been mistreated.

PENSION REVIEW

Those who administer the pension system should have early access to the list of released employees. Presumably, persons who opted earlier for retirement have already been covered. But now additional retirements may impend as a result of outright dismissal. Estimated figures on their pension and continuing benefits will have to be prepared for transmission to them when they hear the news of their plight.

Additionally, other released employees should be told in their exit interviews of their vested status and expectations for pension eligibility in the future, along with their options for lump-sum or annuity settlement.

The pension administrators should have all this material ready by T-Day (Transition Day).

PERSONNEL REVIEW

Once the transition plan has been agreed on, the personnel department picks up the position list and people list. Working from these it must determine the salary ranges of new or changed positions, the salaries to be given to individuals changing jobs, and the payments to be made to departees.

To arrive at salary ranges for a new or changed job, a matter of prime importance to the person affected, Personnel first obtains from those who have introduced the changes a thumbnail job description. From this a provisional job evaluation or job grading is arrived at. Later, with more time and facts available, a fuller description and a more exact determination can be made. For the present, the first-approximation slotting permits arriving at a salary range for the new or changed job. With this in hand it is possible to arrive at a prospective salary for the proposed incumbent. Desirably, promotions to higher-ranked jobs will be accompanied by an increase in pay;

simple lateral transfers may or may not be. And if, earlier on, the granting of merit raises had been deferred in anticipation of the reorganization, these may now be brought back into the picture.

All this analysis is important to the preservation of the ongoing integrity of the salary system. After the transition is over, the company must persist on an even keel, with an internally consistent salary schedule. The chair-shuffling that accompanies reorganization cannot be permitted to disturb salary equities. For example, say two departments are combined into one. The manager of this combined department may seem to be eligible for a higher evaluation and a higher salary range, with an accompanying increase in pay. However, in the cold objective view of job evaluation, the combined position may rank no higher than those it replaces. The incumbent may be eligible for an advance within an existing range, and again maybe not. Similarly, a supervisory position stripped of half its employees may suffer no change in evaluation or grade. Its general requirements remain the same. The incumbent is safe. Only by analyzing each change in terms of the system's rules can change effects be objectively determined.

In a smaller company where no formal evaluation or grading system is in effect, decisions still have to be made on the salaries of people occupying new or changed positions. Here the ex post facto results must be kept in mind. Not "Must I do something for this person today?" but "Where will this person and this person's job fit into the overall picture six months from today?" must govern decisions.

We have spoken of new or changed positions. What of people promoted, transferred, or demoted to existing positions? Salary administration must review their pay histories, as well as company policy, to determine if they are eligible for an increase in pay, no increase, or a decrease.

As an output of all this analysis there results an expanded people list for retained employees. For those experiencing any change in position it stipulates the effect on their pay. This expansion may be seen as an extension, for those affected, of the people list shown in Chapter 10, a right-hand side paste-on, so to speak. An example is shown in Figure 11.1.

The revised list serves a number of purposes. For Payroll it is authorization for salary changes. For people being informed of their own change it is a source of essential financial data. For those who will be figuring the overall cost and savings of the change it is a major input.

In the case of executives and managers who have been apprised in advance of changes in their own status this information will have been worked out earlier on a piecemeal basis. It provides a strong

Figure 11.1

Retained Employees

Present Position	Present Position	Present Position	New or Changed Position	New or Changed Position
Salary Amount	Last Increase		Salary Amount	Eff. Date
	Amount	Date		

Figure 11.2

Separated Employees

Last Date		Salary			Separation Pay			Accumulated Vacation Pay					Total Payment	Monthly Pension Amount	Notes
								This Year		Next Year					
Worked	Paid	Amount	Last Incr.	Date	Years Worked	Weeks Paid	Amount	Amount	Days Due	Days This Year	Days Paid For	Amount			

Note: Provisions of this form depend on circumstances. For example, the total departure payment may be modified by unused sick leave pay, holiday pay, returnable deposits, outstanding expense accounts, lump-sum settlements of accumulated pension, and money owed the company for personal phone calls and personal charges to company credit cards.

affirmation of their own status to those who must guide subordinate moves.

After the dust has settled, Personnel will obtain more comprehensive job descriptions and perform more meticulous job evaluations or gradings. Even the executive of a small company with no formal system of salary management will want to review the assignments to see if they still make sense. And though some revisions may be made, it is likely that familiarity with the positions as a whole will have led to fairly consistent results.

A second occupation of Personnel is to establish the financial arrangements for each person leaving the company. This is done in pursuance of guidelines and policies as to severance pay and its cognates that govern the reorganization dismissals. It requires an inspection of each person's company history as a basis for the various outlays available on employment termination. Where a large number of employees are involved, foresight may enable the computer to carry out these calculations.

For this group a different right-hand addendum is made to the People List (see Figure 11.2). It too may serve as a basis for authorizations to Payroll to have checks prepared. Additionally it supplies the thing people most need to be told when losing their job: How much money do I have coming?

Beyond this Personnel will have a great deal more to do—especially with exit interviews—but all this comes later.

While our discussion may seem to apply mainly to salaried positions, hourly jobs may also be caught up in change. They may be subject to different guidelines and policies, to union contract clauses, and to separate job evaluation systems. Nevertheless they too must be treated with the same care as salaried positions. Whether paid by the month or by the hour, employees are deeply concerned with the specifics of their income. They want to know where they stand and what they can look forward to, and they deserve to be treated with impartial concern for their needs.

FACILITIES

While personnel people are sorting out salary and related effects, others are working on physical facilities. With a reorganization often comes a moving of employees from one desk or office to another, a combination or separation of departments, a consolidation of work areas, a moving of equipment, which may occur in office, shop, or laboratory. In the office, desks, files, telephones, computer terminals, and miscellaneous furniture may have to be relocated. Vice President Williams has inherited the Founder's desk and where he goes it goes.

Discontinued environmentalist Morgan's files of government correspondence have to be moved to the law department. The entire mail-
order receipt department has to transfer from the sales department's
floors to the controller's.

These physical transfers cannot of course be made overnight. On
the other hand no one wants the equipment relocation to drag on
forever like the tail of a comet. People who are moving to a new
position ought to be in place, with their secretary and their files and
their VDT and their own ficus and telephone number, as quickly as
possible so there will be no caesura in their work rhythm.

Usually there is a facilities manager, under one title or another,
who is in charge of such moves. To this person the Planner provides
a confidential list of departmental and individual vacancies or relocations. Putting these into a house-moving sequence so that one area
has always been made empty before its next occupant is moved in
may take considerable study and ingenuity. The facilities manager
spreads floor plans on the drafting table and begins to compare them
with the change descriptions.

Once the changes have been made public everyone affected will,
as mentioned, be impatient to get people physically assembled in
their new locations. But this will not, in any major reorganization,
be done in a day. It is one thing to rearrange 1,000 people on an
organization chart; it is quite another to do it in their working quarters. The facilities manager has to work out a game plan in advance,
then play it over what may turn out to be weeks.

In doing so the manager must arrange for laborers to do the lifting;
painters, carpenters, electricians, and carpet installers, if partitions
are to be arranged; telephone and computer technicians to rewire
numbers and terminals; and perhaps even, if the work is to be done
at night to avoid total daytime chaos, extra security. A consolidation
of locations, such as sales offices, may even require planning for in-
tercity furniture movers.

All of this means that the physical reorganization needs as much
forethought as the personnel one. Therefore, as an adjunct to the chart
changes the Planner may convene a group to assist the facilities manager in new layouts. Where do departments logically belong to fulfill
their new relationships? Are some of them likely to expand, so that
additional space should be available for them? Is there a desirable
pattern for their internal layout? Is there a company practice regarding eligibility for private or semiprivate offices, and if so where
will these be located? Can condensation of the payroll release space
that will either no longer need to be rented or can be made available
to new occupants? Will space contracts in a rental office have to be
renegotiated? Will additional space be needed, as may happen in a

consolidation of formerly separate centers? Is there a priority list of changes? These are questions to which the facilities manager must have answers from the advisory group.

As immediate outputs before T-Day the facilities manager will prepare two sets of information. The first is a schedule, perhaps in the form of a PERT chart, of all moves to be made, whether in parallel or in sequence, with approximate timing. The second is a preliminary estimate of the one-shot cost of the moves along with changes in ongoing occupancy expense.

All this takes thought and time and it affects how quickly the new organization gets its wheels on the ground. Accordingly, the Planner should get it into the scheduling process as soon as possible.

PUBLIC RELATIONS

Interest in the reorganization is not confined to those participating in it. A small interoffice change in a large company or a large shuffle in a small one may not capture the attention of outside communities, but significant changes in a large company will. For example, outsiders like and may need to know what is going on when a large company:

- Absorbs an acquisition
- Substantially reduces its work force
- Consolidates factories or offices
- Replaces a number of executives and upper-level managers
- Discontinues (or adds) lines of business
- Changes its orientation, from functional to product, or vice versa.

They need to be told, and to be told they must be identified. For example, a reorganization may be of general interest to:

- Local government groups, including the mayor or county commissioners
- Bankers doing business with the company
- The local and national press and TV
- Financial analysts
- Trade publications
- Trade associations.

Still further information may be offered to recipients having a more focused interest in dealing with the company's operations or with some of its specific employees. For example:

- The Unemployment Compensation Claims Offices and Job Service should be notified if a large number of departures is expected.
- Suppliers should be told of changes in purchasing personnel.
- Certain government agencies should be advised of changes in the people they contact.
- Customers should know of changes in sales personnel or location.
- Unions whose members are affected may be privately contacted by whoever normally deals with their officers. An understanding of what is happening may prevent difficulties.
- Consultants may be advised of changes in the positions they normally contact, as may outside counsel, auditing firms, and local community agencies.
- Advertising agencies working for the company need to know of changes in the people engaged with them.

Some of this communication can be spread with a press release or form letter at the time of reorganization. Some (a talk with the union president or the mayor, for instance) on a one-to-one confidential basis just before. Some—the press release, for instance—may mention not only restructuring itself but also its expected effect on earnings, if the company thinks this of interest. Some—the one-to-one talk, for instance—may deal with more limited proportions of the change. But to avoid contradictions and misinformation, all news of the reorganization should be coordinated and approved by the company's public relations officer.

For a few people coaching sessions may be called for. Is the president prepared to reply to telephoned questions from the media? Is the factory manager, whose plant is to be mothballed, equipped to respond to an interview by the local TV station? When the company seems to outsiders to be all a-tremble, that is when a good front is important.

But, it may be said, why publicize at all? And in some cases indeed it may be just as well not to. If this is the company's third reorganization in four years, for example; or if the changes are essentially internal with little impact on employment or the communities engaged with the company.

On the other hand, if massive disemployment results, questions will be raised whether the company desires them or not. And if the reorganization is expected to strengthen the company, only good can come from letting the various publics know that it is under aggressive hard-charging management. So it is best for the company to control the reaction to its reorganization through intelligent communication to all interested.

SECURITY

A contractive reorganization brings along with it some risk in security. Both people and property may be ever so slightly more vulnerable than before.

Job loss ranks high on the emotional trauma list, and in every large group there are a few individuals who can get along with some aspects of it but not with others. Thus with sudden disemployment an employee may not suffer an immediate zeroing down of income. Severance pay, accumulated benefits, and unemployment compensation (if available) help to allay the financial damage, at least for a time. But emotionally the damage may be great. Being fired while others are retained can be shaming. There is, besides a plunge of expectations, a foreclosing of plans, both personal and professional, an emptiness of future. Most people weather such storms, but some thought should be given to the few who cannot. It is not unknown for an embittered and resentful ex-employee to return to the premises with violence in mind. Many ex's will be coming back anyway to settle various questions relating to their termination. Security should be alerted to the possibility of an occasional problem-stricken person.

Property too needs safeguarding. Trying to keep paperwork—customer lists, for example—from moving out the doors is difficult. Employees who had any inkling of a crisis ahead will have abstracted it days or weeks before. Tools and equipment are another matter. A recorder in the pocket, a hand drill in the lunch bucket, a typewriter in the trunk of the car are losses that the company must be prepared either to endure or prevent. In the complete shutdown of a factory a migration of small tools is to be expected and tales of large equipment being passed over a fence or through a window are not unknown. Even the risk of sabotage should not be overlooked. Whether in the machine shop or in the computer room there are opportunities for unhappy employees to leave lasting damage behind them. A closely supervised exit is not without its merits, paranoid though it may seem.

Most employees are, of course, perfectly trustworthy. Nevertheless the pressures of exit may create isolated responses that the security department should be prepared to recognize. The Planner does well to alert the head of that department in advance of the approaching transition.

FINAL APPROVAL

The activities just described have fallen hard on the heels of the preliminary approval of the reorganization plan. That approval was based on a rough-cut proposal that had not yet assumed all its details. Now, as the move begins to jell into its permanent mold, the Initiators must decide if it is suitable for final approval.

The Planner assembles materials for presentation. These include:

1. The original objectives, with an indication as to whether the reorganization does what is necessary to accomplish them.

2. Other desirable actions that have turned up in the course of the investigation—for example, an opportunity to reduce home office order-entry staff by putting more computer terminals in branch offices, to be used by on-hand employees there.

3. The expected financial effects of the reorganization, which will include extraordinary immediate expenses; those increases or decreases in expense that will persist after the change (including long-term savings); and additions or write-off of assets, again those to occur now and those yet to be realized. For the savings some breakdown may be supplied: how much comes from direct payroll, how much from fringes, and how much from personnel-associated variable overhead. Additionally, there may be savings from locational shutdowns and combinations. The amount of future investment and payroll growth that may be precluded by the changes at hand also belongs in this financial section.

4. Head counts before and after reorganization. The assumptions underlying these counts should be stated. For example, does the "before" count include unfilled positions? For that matter, does the "after" count include bona fide unfilled positions? If the company is seasonal, what period of the year do the counts represent? The counts need not cover only the edges of the change. In a reorganization for growth the personnel count may well be extended to show projected employment levels, by category, for six-month periods lying ahead.

5. Organization charts for the pre- and post-change structures.

6. Description of supporting activities that will accompany the change, such as those in public relations, security, and physical rearrangement.

7. The recommended timing and duration of the change process.

The proposal is approved, all the more quickly if the Planner has been able to go to the Initiators during its preparation for informal advice on knotty issues that have come up.

Transition Day is at hand.

Transition Day

12

A TO Z

Transition Day (T-Day) arrives. For reasons already described it is, desirably, a Monday or a Tuesday not preceding a holiday. It is not a day in which large numbers of employees are ensnarled in the month-end closing, annual inventory, or the final draft of next year's budget. It is a day in which full attention can be given to the birthing of the revised organization.

How the transition is handled can have a profound effect on the success of the reorganization. From the company's point of view the purpose is to cut into a new highway without getting lost in the cloverleaf. The transition should be merely a smooth, well-controlled unproblemed change in direction. From the employees' point of view the change of course may be either alarming or rewarding. But if they are to drive through it into increasing productivity it must not be vague or perplexing. T-Day, then, is a crucial interlude between yesterday and tomorrow in the company's history. We are therefore going to examine it in some detail, even to the point of justifiable fussiness. For T-Day, well structured in its particulars, is the day on which all affected members of the organization learn of their changed roles. How do its communications proceed?

Throughout its progress a sequence of steps guided by "talk memos" is repeated at successively descending levels. Each involves an executive, manager, or supervisor, whom for convenience we will refer to generically as "Boss A"—any superior telling a subordinate about the change; and the recipient of the information, whom we will call generically "Employee Z." Employee Z may be superior to other subordinates, and in passing the reorganization information on to them becomes in turn "Boss A" for that purpose. At any level the steps are four in number:

1. Boss A invites Employee Z to Boss A's office and communicates to Employee Z the overall nature of and reasons for the reconstitution of the company structure.
2. Boss A clearly describes what change, if any, will occur in Employee Z's status.
3. Boss A tells Employee Z what to do next. Employee Z leaves Boss A's office.
4. If Employee Z is moving to another department, Boss A phones Employee Z's new boss, who can then invite Z for further elaboration on Z's new job. If not, Boss A calls in the next employee under Boss A for a reiteration of these steps.

In this series we take "Boss A" to be someone below the rank of the president. If the reorganization is company-wide, the vice presidents probably know about it already. It is inconceivable that anything of this magnitude would be sprung on any one of them out of the blue. So each of the vice presidents becomes Boss A in the beginning of our scenario. Once their set of interviews is over their respective subordinates become "Boss A" in interviews with their own employees, who are each "Employee Z."

Let us look at the steps more closely, assuming again that the reorganization is company-wide.

FOUR STEPS

Step I: If none of Boss A's immediate subordinates are directly affected by the changes, they may be called into Boss A's office as a group to be filled in on what is happening. If, however, one or more of them are about to experience a change in status, Boss A calls those people in first, one at a time. (Boss A starts, as a matter of good sense, with Boss A's own secretary. The secretary, affected or not, needs to know what is going on.) In Step I Boss A:

1. Displays and explains abbreviated charts of the old and new company structures, as a general background.
2. Sketches out why the reorganization is occurring and what benefits are expected from it.
3. Presents full charts for the structure of Boss A's piece of the company, which is Employee Z's immediate concern.
4. Explains the changes in Employee Z's own area of Boss A's chart.

All this should be handled as expeditiously as possible since, as Boss A will probably point out, a great many people have yet to be notified, including those under Employee Z.

In one case, all of Step I may be omitted if Employee Z is to leave the company. In this event Employee Z does not have anything to gain from being told the details of the reorganization beyond the fact that it is underway.

Step II: In Step II of Boss A's succinct interview with Employee Z, Boss A elucidates what Employee Z's status will be after the reorganization. This status may fall into any of several situations:

1. No change.
2. Lateral transfer to another position which is (a) still reporting to Boss A, or (b) under another boss.
3. Promotion to another position which again may be (a) still under Boss A, or (b) under another boss.
4. Demotion to another position (a) still under Boss A, or (b) under another boss.
5. Severance from the organization, either (a) on this same day, or (b) on a specified future date.

There are thus a number of alternative statuses available, but only one applies to the specific Employee Z being addressed.

Boss A then informs Employee Z of any change in salary that Employee Z will receive if remaining under Boss A, along with its effective date. If Employee Z is being moved to a position under another boss, say Boss B, then Boss B will handle salary notification in an entry interview to be described shortly.

Boss A also informs Employee Z of any change in physical location that Z will be making.

Boss A additionally provides Employee Z with a job description if Z is remaining under A in a new position. This may be one already available or that thumbnail temporary description put together for evaluation purposes.

Employee Z now knows in a general way about the overall reorganization, and in a specific way about its effect on him or her in its reporting, financial, operational, and locational features.

Step III: In Step III of the interview Boss A tells Employee Z what to do next. Again there are alternative actions depending on the change in status.

1. No change: Z may return to his or her workplace. If there are employees reporting to Z, Z then informs them individually of the changes and how each of them will be affected, repeating the three steps of Boss A's se-

quence. To assist Z in doing this, Boss A gives Z a packet of talk memos previously prepared for this purpose.

2. Promotion, lateral transfer, or demotion to another position, still under Boss A: If this position has employees reporting to it, Boss A introduces Z to Z's new immediate subordinates as a group, explaining what has become of their former (if any) boss, that Z is their new boss, and that Z will cover them on the details of the changes. Z, now in the role of Boss A to these employees, then enters on the three steps with them.

3. Promotion, lateral transfer, or demotion to another position under a different boss, Boss B: Boss A tells Employee Z of this change and explains that Boss B will phone Z for an entry interview describing the new position and preparing Z, if the new position has subordinates, for an introduction to its remaining employees, with whom Z will then be repeating the three steps of notification, assisted by a set of talk memos provided by Boss B.

4. Severance: Boss A tells Employee Z that Z's services will not be required in the new organization. If Z is to leave on the same day, Z is told that the personnel department will arrange for an exit interview. If it is desired that Z continue to work until some future date—for example, to assist in transition or to help close down a facility—Z is told that expected future departure date, with the understanding that eligibility for severance pay, for example, depends on Z's accomplishing these purposes satisfactorily. If Z is a boss, A tells Z that A will take care of notifying Z's subordinates, either in person or through Z's successor.

Step IV: Having completed the first three steps with each employee Z, Boss A so reports by phone to the Planner's staff who are keeping track of progress. Boss A then phones the various Boss B's to whom some of his or her employees will be transferring so that they can arrange entry interviews with the Z's who are joining them. Boss A also contacts the personnel department, giving the go-ahead to proceed with exit interviews with any Z's who are being terminated.

Boss A then leans back in the chair and, in the role of "Boss B," prepares to phone any Employee Z's who are being transferred into his or her domain.

ENTRY INTERVIEW

Boss B, interviewing an Employee Z who is joining B's next level downward, covers several points similar to those in previous talks.

• Z's new title is stated.
• Z's change in salary, if any, is stated along with its effective date.
• Z is told of the new status of Z's predecessor, if any, on Z's new position.
• Z is shown where Z's position fits on B's portion of the organization chart and what positions will report to Z.

- Z is introduced to the occupants of these positions (some of whom may have just been transferred in to Z's supervision).

- Z then goes through the four steps with them. In some of these interviews Z takes the role of Boss A. In others Z takes the role of Boss B.

AMBIANCE

Despite the peremptory sound of this sequence, the interviews are not conducted in the manner of, say, authoritarian Prussians in the movies—"You vill report to der oberhauptman und you vill do as he says!" What has been harshly and mechanistically outlined here should, and probably will, occur in an atmosphere of human warmth. The Boss A/B role regards the changes being made as reinforcing to the company's future, and hence beneficial to all that future's employees. A sense prevails of opportunity unlocked.

To persons receiving a promotion the boss expresses hearty congratulations. To those leaving on a lateral transfer the boss expresses hope that the new position will offer better potential than the old one. To persons coming in to the department from other positions the boss expresses a warm, friendly welcome. To persons being demoted or fired the boss expresses not exactly sympathy, which may only encourage unproductive emotional response, but something more like a sense of inevitability and finality. And each interview concludes on an optimistic note, even one falsely so, if necessary, for the wounded. Who knows, some of them may get rehired or repromoted some day. All the interviews should be as expeditious as possible. Even to ask if a change is acceptable to Z is to open up possibilities for time-consuming discussion. It should be assumed that Z goes along with and concurs in the change, even if not enthusiastically. There will be time for more selling tomorrow. The main point on T-Day is to get everyone notified. This should not take more than five or ten minutes per person. Very roughly, if each upper-level boss has say, ten people to talk to, all the bosses on a level should finish their interviews in an hour and a half. This means that some six levels, surely the most one should expect in any organizational entity, should be covered in a long day. The interviews may seem, however friendly, abrupt; but there will be plenty of succeeding days for each boss to organize the intricacies of a department.

NOTIFICATION SUPPORT

The interviewing and notifying process proceeds rapidly only if it is well-prepared for. To this end the Planner or the Planner's staff provides each boss with a folder of supporting data. This folder includes:

- A T-Day agenda (see Figure 12.1) summarizing the sequence of events and persons to be talked to. This serves as both a tracking device and a checklist.
- Charts showing the before and after company-wide organization in outline. These stay with the boss, to be shown to each person interviewed.
- A clip for each retained employee to be talked to, consisting of: (a) A talk memo (Figure 12.2) to remind Boss A of what must be conveyed to Employee Z; (b) A job description of the new position (if any), to be given to Employee Z; (c) An organization chart of Z's area if Z will be a boss; and (d) A set of similar clips if Z has subordinates to be talked to.

SHORT CUTS

Where does all this material come from? The Planner issues it, assisted by the personnel department. It may seem that in a large company this is a daunting task. But it need not be, for several reasons.

For some employees extended talk memos are not required. For example, in addressing released employees, Boss A, referring to the agenda, need only say (as humanely as possible) that with the reorganization there will be no place in the company for them, and their last day worked will be such-and-such. All other information on their departure they will receive from the personnel department in an exit interview.

For employees remaining on the same job it is only necessary to show them the new chart and tell them their job is unaffected.

If talks with changed-status employees have already been taken care of, the talk with those left may be handled in a group meeting. In fact, there are apt to be departments not directly touched by reorganization, and in them, too, a group meeting for general description of the change may suffice.

Even when employees are transferred from one department to an existing job in another, the Boss A talk consists in essence of saying "so long" and the Boss B talk is a "welcome aboard!"

None of this requires much paperwork at the moment, nor should it take much time.

Some of the work may even have been done ahead. The computer may have been enlisted to prepare people lists with names, job titles, dates, and salary changes. Many of the bosses will have been engaged in the get-together in which details were worked out. Given an outline, they may prepare their own talk-memos.

Subsetting the transition also helps. For example, in a very large company the reorganization may be compartmentalized into cells. A

T-DAY AGENDA FOR BOSS "A"

1. Talk to the following employees remaining in department with change of status.

   Name
   Name
   Name

2. Talk to the following employees being transferred to another area of the company and telephone Boss "B" to call employee for interview.

Employee	Boss "B"	Telephone No.
Name	Name	xxxx
Name	Name	xxxx

3. Talk to the following employees leaving through termination.

   Name
   Name

   (a) Telephone Personnel to arrange exit interview. Report any problems arising in notification.

4. Talk to the following employees remaining in department with no change in status.

   Name
   Name

5. Telephone in and talk to the following employees transferring into department from other areas of company (after receiving go-ahead from previous boss).

Employee	Telephone No.	Oĸ'd
Name	xxxx	☐

6. Telephone Planner when all interviews have been completed.

Figure 12.1

<u>TALK MEMO</u>

Employee: <u>J. A. Smith</u>

Smile and ask Smith to take a seat. Then . . .

1.   Explain that the company is being reorganized in order to reduce
       overhead, to attain a better competitive position, and to absorb
       the subsidiary recently acquired. Show before and after organi-
       zation charts. Show before and after charts of your own organi-
       zation.

2.   Tell Smith that as part of this change Smith is being promoted from
       Section Head, Complaints Correspondence, to a newly-created
       position of Manager, Complaints Investigation, in charge of the
       positions shown on the new chart. Give Smith a job description
       for the new position and an organization chart for Smith's new
       enclave.

3.   Tell Smith this change will be effective the fifteenth of this month.
       Smith's salary will increase from $XOOO per month to $XYOO per
       month, also effective the fifteenth.

4.   Tell Smith that the people who are to report directly to Smith will
       be introduced to Smith today so that Smith can talk to each of them.
       Until then Smith should maintain confidentiality.

5.   Give Smith a folder of Talk Memos to assist in this further com-
       munication. The folder will contain a list of the people who will
       report to Smith, their salary changes, if any, their position titles,
       and preliminary job descriptions (which Smith will want to refine
       after getting the new department organized).

6.   Congratulate Smith and tell Smith that after T-Day you will be able
       to discuss the new job in more detail.

Call in the next person on your agenda.

Figure 12.2

subsidiary, a major division, a factory, a large away-from-headquar-
ters office may each work out its own reorganization with its own
Planner, under the guidance of objectives issued from above. In this
way the number of interviews and the paperwork for an individual
cell can be held to manageable numbers. Subsetting also permits
transition interviews to be held in parallel, on the same day, at those
locations that are scattered around the country.
   A further means of holding the interviews within bounds is the

postponement of everything possible to subsequent days. Employee questions about physical location and rearrangement can be taken up later. How new or changed departments will tackle their mission can be handled later. This is a day for helping people by quickly telling them who is where, so that they will not spend days worrying about how they stand.

Yet another means for simplifying the process is to notify all key executives, managers, and supervisors the day before the bulk of the other changes. Talk-memos are used here, too, just to be sure all essentials get covered; but their number, at these upper levels of the pyramid, is smaller. Moreover, acceptance of new assignments at this level is crucial. Though the changes may have been worked out in previous meetings, willingness to go along is worth confirming a day in advance. No cut and dried military reassignment is being imposed. Rather, an offer is being extended, an opportunity. It is well to know, before the T-Day rush, that it is being picked up.

A further preparatory measure is an advance class for key bosses on *how* to conduct the impending interviews. Without getting into all the specifics of changes, the leader of such a meeting emphasizes interview climate, how to deal with emotions, how to conduct terminations, the need to keep the interview on track, and the format of the papers that guide the interview. With this background the various Boss A's and Boss B's can keep the transition perking along with a minimum of lost time. Also, their full knowledge of how to handle the change permits the talk-memos to be reduced to little more than a form on which blanks are filled in appropriately for each employee, along with stereotyped reminder notes for what the boss must discuss. Condensation, segmentation, and constraint keep T-Day to its single purpose: rapid communication.

MASS NOTIFICATION

The procedures herein described work well and are in fact essential at most levels of the organization. But many ground-floor departments are so heavily populated with employees that individual notification is neither practicable nor necessary. Often these areas are occupied by nonexempts, whether on salary or wage. For example, they may include such jobs as chip-sealers in an electronics factory, order receivers in a large mail-order house, clerks in a retail chain, policy enterers in an insurance company. It is safe to say that their occupants have little interest in the overall structure of the company. But they do care about the job they work on and the supervisor they report to. So they should not be ignored. They should know anything about T-Day that has a bearing on them.

For a few of them individual interviews will be called for—the check processor who is going to be made group leader, for example. For the rest a bulletin-board announcement will in most cases tell them what they need to know.

But a special case occurs when large numbers of these nonexempts are going to be asked to report to a new location. Many companies take pains to inform such employees of the move in full detail. By letter and by group meeting they outline provisions for job retention, counselling, assistance in relocation, and financing the move. Merrill Lynch & Company, planning to shift some 3,000 back office employees from New York City to outlying sites, gave the participants two years advance notice to permit personal arrangements to be made with minimum shock.[1]

Small jobs should not be overlooked when big changes are afoot.

PROBLEM EVENTS

Since nothing works perfectly, a few problems are bound to arise on T-Day. Some may be events that should have been foreseen but were not. Some may be difficulties that bosses can handle on the spot. (After all, that's how they got to be bosses, knowing how to deal with the unexpected.) Others may have to be referred back to a higher level of authority or perhaps to the Planner. For some examples:

Outright refusal: "What, me work for that creep? Never! I'm staying right where I am."

Resignation: "But that's a demotion! I'm quitting."

Fright: "I know it's a promotion, and I appreciate it. But I don't honestly think I can handle that job."

Threat: "It's because of my age, isn't it? I'm seeing my lawyer."

Undercut: "Well, gee, I wish I'd known about this promotion sooner. I've just accepted a job with X Company and I was going to give you my notice next Monday."

Missing: Employee Z is not on hand to be talked to, off sick.

Occupied: Employee Z has an outside auditor in the office and can't be interrupted, everything thereby being thrown behind schedule.

Timid: Boss A suddenly finds self emotionally unable to deal with firing people.

Afterthought: Last-minute realization that Engineer Z, scheduled to be fired, is the only person who understands the piping on the recovery still.

Emotions: General manager, learning that not he but a colleague has been made vice president, slams door behind him on his way out in an unanticipated rage. His secretary, fearing loss of own job, has to be escorted to company nurse.

Gunjumping: Employee Z leaves Boss A's office and announces changes, some incorrectly, to all employees within ear or phone shot, thereby creating both dismay and total misunderstanding.

Carelessness: Boss A ignores talk memos, with result that some employees leave interview ill-informed, others misinformed.

Slowdown: Boss A, a loquacious, sociable person, takes a half-hour for each interview, throwing all subsequent ones off schedule.

Emergency: Boss A is called out on T-Day morning to make a hasty and essential visit to a troublesome customer.

Errors and Omissions: People Lists (the basis for preparing talk memos), agendas, and charts turn out not to include the voice-communications expert, eight word-processor operators, and a cell biologist, all of whom were hired in the last week; nor four employees on pregnancy leave; but do still include fifteen people who resigned for various reasons in the last two weeks. Lists also have failed to include all salary increases approved in the last week but not yet entered on salary tape. They also have neglected to consider the future status of fifteen part-time lab workers and three interns.

A number of these problems can be prevented or at least minimized by discussing their possibility in the pre–T-Day meetings for bosses. At that time preventive or corrective measures can also be suggested. For example, if a Boss A is suddenly called away from the office or shop on T-Day, arrangements can be made for his or her superior to take over the talks.

Other difficulties will have been anticipated in advance. For example, say a proposed move is that of Employee Z from the position Manager of the Chicago factory to General Manufacturing Manager in the headquarters office. This might be anticipatorially and confidentially covered in an advance visit. Similarly, a proposed reshuffling of managers among sales offices may have to be handled by calling them all in for a sales conference and notifying them individually then. Why not just inform them all in an open meeting? Because it may turn out that some of them cannot make the move at this time.

By and large, forethought permits dealing with most problems that may come up. And as we said, most executives, managers, and supervisors in their roles of Boss A or B are quite able to take care of them, sometimes by ad hoc revisions of minor elements in the plan. These they promptly report back to the Planner or the Planner's staff.

WRAP-UP

At the end of T-Day the Planner should have a thorough knowledge of how the transition talks have come out. During the talks there have been phone feedbacks on progress. The Planner has been marking off on a log those areas that have been completed, layer by layer down through the organization. Problem events have been recorded, together with what has been done or will have to be done on account of them. Where it has been found impossible to execute a proposed move, Personnel has been notified so that corrections may be made in, for example, planned salary changes. Public Relations has been informed of progress so that it may release news of the change to the company's various publics and alert the president for possible media interviews.

If this transition has been going on simultaneously at both headquarters and branch locations, the Planner will be relying on phone calls from managers or planners around the country for progress reports, some widely scattered on the clock because of time zone differences.

When local branches—factories, offices, warehouses, service centers, or stores, for example—are being closed, special measures must often be taken by the local manager almost at once. They may include notification not only to the mayor, the union, and the media but also to utilities, the Job Service and unemployment offices, insurance companies (if not handled from headquarters offices), materials shippers, transportation companies, the post office, building managers (if the quarters are leased), and contract service suppliers. Security must be arranged for. Provision must be made for entry and control of persons temporarily retained for clean-up, maintenance, mothballing, and preparing the site for shutdown. Some of this is set in motion on Transition Day and some in the days immediately following. The Planner will also require a progress report on the performance of these activities.

As soon as possible the Planner reports back to the Initiators on the degree of completion of the first day of transition. For all the participants the real work of company improvement now begins.

NOTE

1. *New York Times*, 15 Oct. 1985.

13

Aftermath

A gilded coach is not made by waving a wand at a pumpkin. It is painstakingly constructed by a host of artisans plying trades unknown to wand wavers. Nor is a company reborn by a transition day. All that happens on that day is a notification that the wand has been waved. For the reorganization to become a working reality much more must be accomplished.

Some of this hammer-and-nails work is procedural, some is more creative. The procedural tasks are not the less important for being commonplace. In fact, without them the attainment of larger goals may be delayed. And while Initiators of great moves may be ignorant or perhaps scornful of petty details, Planners who must get the re-organization quickly completed cannot take them for granted. For every small chore there must be a person responsible for doing it by a stipulated date.

The Planner must set up a laundry list of activities and become an expediter of them. But surely, it may be said, all the follow-up tasks are self-evident and those employees involved are fully aware of them. Not necessarily. For one thing, reorganizations are not part of routine business. The typical employee, if fortunate, is inexperienced in them. The load of work they bring may be far beyond the day-to-day round of duties that is normally handled. For a second thing, the reorgan-ization itself may have left people in jobs they are not wholly familiar with. It may even have reduced staff at a time when staff work is going to be temporarily overwhelming. The Planner must organize follow-up activities with the same orderly care as those of T-Day. And what are these mundane pursuits that should not be taken for granted?

Let's look at some of them before going on to the more creative and constructive aspects of getting reorganized.

EXIT INTERVIEWS

One of the first things to be done is to schedule formal exit interviews for those employees leaving the company. Normally these are conducted by the personnel department. Who is to be talked to depends somewhat on the circumstances. Thus the release of several hundred nonexempts or hourly workers holding fairly routine jobs may permit no individual interviews at all. Though this is undoubtedly abrupt and impersonal treatment, sheer numbers preclude having a chat with each employee. The financial conditions of departure—severance pay, benefits continuation, pension data, and the like may have to be communicated in a letter.

Some of these employees and others above them on the ladder may require additional, more specific attention. For example, it may be necessary before authorizing departure payments and accumulated pay, to obtain return of a company car, keys, credit cards, company pass or I.D., company manuals, instruments and tools, devices (calculators, recorders, and tapes, for instance), books, and other company property. The employee may need to be told what expiration date will govern club and society memberships and periodicals. Did the employee participate in an annual bonus scheme? If so, how will the bonus be prorated, if at all, and when will it be paid? If the employee was attending classes with tuition paid by the company, does the agreement to pay still stand? Some employees may need to be reminded not to transmit confidential company information to new employers. Others may want to know the company's policy on references.

The availability of special arrangements may also be described in the interview, including such provisions as:

• Resumé service
• Stenographic assistance
• Telephone answering
• Temporary office quarters
• Orientation classes
• Outplacement consultation.

As a matter of prudence the interviewer will make a note of any out-of-the-ordinary emotional manifestations or grievances that crop up. Someone should keep in touch with a particularly distressed employee.

For many of these activities Personnel will have had to make advance preparation—for example, getting the requisite financial data together or lining up resumé and counselling services. It will also have follow-up chores—returning company possessions to their respective departments, possibly notifying credit card companies of people who have not returned cards or did not show up for the interview.

These activities require planning as to both time and content. In many companies they are eased by the use of standardized checklists. Nevertheless, if the number of departures is large, the Planner will want to be sure that Personnel has prepared itself to deal with them.

EVALUATIONS

Not all companies employ a standardized position evaluation or salary ranking system, but in those that do reorganization is apt to wash in a flood of work to be done. New or changed jobs are almost certain to be created and each must be fitted in its proper place among all others in the pay structure.

As mentioned, abbreviated, prospective job descriptions and approximate evaluations and salary rankings will likely have been made for guidance on T-Day. Now these must be refined to permanent form.

With assistance from those affected the evaluator obtains expanded, more exact position descriptions. On the basis of these an evaluation then determines each job's ranking with respect to others. And from this, in turn, Salary Administration identifies the salary range that goes with the job. This may differ somewhat from the pre–T-Day estimate, and is communicated to the supervisor of the job in question.

The new job descriptions are useful in different ways. In their preparation itself the supervisor and perhaps even the position incumbent can work out the content and scope of positions showing up for the first time on the organization chart. Some of these positions are what is left after responsibilities have been split away from previous ones; some are a combination of antecedent jobs; and some are new introductions. Clearly describing them helps to pin down what the employee is expected to do. They thus serve as both an instruction and a reference. After the reorganization has settled down into its revised structure supervisors will employ the descriptions in appraisal sessions with subordinates to be sure that everything originally contemplated is indeed being accomplished.

To get new job descriptions, evaluations, and salary status quickly in place is a must in the T-Day follow up. It is personally important to employees to know their financial status more exactly than in the estimate cited on T-Day; and it is important to the company, first, to have job rankings firmed up and secondly, to have comprehensive job descriptions to guide the formative stages of the new structure.

PERSONNEL RECORDS

Large organizations set in motion many behind-the-scenes processes that are largely unappreciated by anyone except those performing them. One of these is the updating of the personnel records that are maintained for each employee.

For starters, the individual files on terminated employees must be pulled and supplied with the date and reason for termination, together with any accompanying notes pertaining to the individual.

For retained employees there may be entries for new department, new position title, and salary change. Where geographic transfers have occurred, change of address and phone number are also entered. Depending on company predilection for thoroughness even further data may be keyed in: name of supervisor, for example, or record of company assets (such as cars) in the employees' possession, along with company-paid memberships.

Separately the pension tapes or discs are acquiring entries for newly retired employees as well as those who have been terminated with vesting. The salary administration department is updating its individual records for employees to show newly approved salary changes, and similarly, the payroll department is recording authorizations for payment.

Some of these changes have fallout in other areas. If there is, for example, a company medical department that keeps track of employee treatments or periodic physical examinations, it will want a list of names to be removed from its active record. If there is a communications department that mails releases or company publications to employees' homes, it will need a current address list. If employee I.D. cards specify department or authorize access to restricted areas, new ones have to be issued.

Considering the volume of records work to be done in addition to exit interviews the personnel department carries a heavy load immediately after T-Day. For this reason any contemplated force reductions in that department are better deferred till the crest of the wave has passed.

PHYSICAL RELOCATION

Preparations for rearrangement of space and facilities—even the moving of an employee from one desk to another—should be made in advance. But upon completion of T-Day they should be rechecked. They do not always work out as expected. The manager of telephone solicitation, for example, has quit rather than be placed under the marketing manager, and until a replacement is found the proposed move of the telephone callers to another location is on hold. The newly appointed housewares manager wants her buyers in semiprivate offices, not in a bull-pen plan. The vice president of customer relations balks at being assigned an office looking out on a side street. T-Day not only embodies change, it creates further change.

To adapt to these needs the facilities manager reworks the moving schedule; then the physical relocations get underway. They may stretch out for weeks, and the Planner keeps in touch with them, for they as much as anything are essential to getting the reorganization airborne.

In the meantime some very trifling matters must be taken care of almost daily. The receptionist has to be kept updated on where people are located and also, perhaps, on the names of people no longer present. Say a visitor wants to speak to Jim Smith, who is gone from the fold; what is the receptionist to tell her? Another wants to talk to the buyer of printed forms; does the receptionist know who now occupies this position?

Similar information must be made available to telephone operators. And of course the phone directory will have to be revised repeatedly until everybody is in place.

Meanwhile, down in the mailroom, the boss keeps in touch with every change of location as it occurs, so that the messengers know where to dispatch incoming mail. This may seem insignificant, yet certainly no one wants company business to be retarded by a day because letters have to be rerouted. Remembering the mailroom is part of even the most massive reorganization.

And then there is the night clean-up crew to be reassigned....

ACCOUNTING

Reorganization creates immediate follow-up duties, both small and large, for the accounting department.

A small, but immediate requirement is to revise the authorized approvals list. With the occurrence of new, combined, or discontinued positions and incumbents comes a revision of who is accredited to approve, for example, appropriation requests, expense accounts, and payment on invoices.

Beyond this comes revision of the chart of accounts. Where the reorganization is prompted by an acquisition or merger this may be a large undertaking indeed, one that will require its own timetable for accomplishment. With lesser, internal reorganization the new chart of accounts probably reflects only the redirection of expenses to new departmental targets. The change may, however, have far-reaching implications. For example, with the new chart may come reallocations of overhead. The closing of regional factories or offices shifts general overhead to those that remain. Even the transfer of a department—say Distribution from the sales to the operations division—may affect the overhead that department bears. And as these overhead figures sift down to products or services there may be a seeming change in ultimate cost to produce and ship. Such a change may in turn trigger new views on the profitability of lines of product or service, resulting in altered emphasis in "portfolio" management. An extensive change in the chart of accounts is far more than the production of new charge numbers on a list. Accountants, strategic planners, and marketing managers will want to study its effects. For example, by eliminating facilities that made less-profitable product lines, the company may have also eliminated those lines' overhead absorption, with a corresponding increase in allocation to more profitable ones. Say the company thought it was the low-cost producer of the latter and now finds that it is not: What does this tell us about the low-cost producer concept, and also about the long-range effects of reorganization? Such swings in the weight of overhead cannot always be anticipated in the financial analysis accompanying reorganization proposals. They should therefore be examined in follow-up revisions of the chart of accounts. Arbitrary though they may seem to be, they may, if not fully understood, sway decisions on marketing emphasis and pricing.

With the chart of accounts revised, the way is clear for generation of new budgets. These incorporate not only the revised department structure, but also, where there has been a reduction in work force, the expected lowering of indirect expense. Budget preparation is usually a major undertaking, even when this year's is only a modification of last year's. When it follows a reorganization, it becomes doubly complicated because not only has the network of charges been regrouped, but the content too has changed. New cost centers have arisen and old ones have disappeared. Even in departments retaining their identity, payroll, travel, telephone, and many other expenses may have been sunk to lower levels by reorganization. Unless these are recognized, the budget becomes meaningless for future control— it is only a measure of performance against the past.

With a reorganization oriented to growth, on the other hand, budgeted amounts may provide for expected increases in personnel-associated costs. Curiously, in such cases actual charges well below budget may indicate inadequate performance; the department is not growing as fast as was desired.

In any case, budgeting the new organization may not be easy. Almost certainly a reorganization is undertaken with an expectation of some significant and measurable impact on profit. If it includes a retreat from certain sales regions or an intrusion into new ones, if it is predicated on the addition or dropping of present lines, then it may be expected to influence sales and hence the sales budget. If it initiates a reduction in outlays, it is intended to influence the expense budget. So to reconstruct the budget with new sales income and new expenses for running the business in order to arrive at the hoped-for new operating profit is an out-of-the-ordinary budget undertaking.

Budget revision may depend on timing. If the reorganization occurs toward the end of the fiscal year, a budget revision for the remaining months may hardly be worth the effort. Concentrating on next year's budget would be better. If the reorganization occurs shortly after the beginning of the fiscal year, however, revision is almost mandatory. How else is the postrevision period to be controlled?

Budget revision may also depend on the scope of the reorganization. Reorganization of a few departments for improved performance may require only modest budget review. One that affects sales or introduces a whole new internal structure—changing from functional to product grouping of divisions and departments, for example, or assimilating a new acquisition—simply makes the old budget obsolete.

Budget revision is no small thing, and it is a hard imposition to lay on those who are preoccupied with getting the organization up and running in all its new relationships—something like asking a runner to change his shirt as he starts off from the blocks—but it has to be faced.

SYSTEMS

Sitting not far from the company's computer programmers is a group known as systems analysts. Their job is to schematize the various entries, recordings, interactions, flows, and issuances of information that accompany and sometimes initiate company actions. Such systems may, for example, codify the complete processing of a sales order, from initial entry through stock withdrawal, inventory

balancing, shipping instructions, to accounts receivable. In doing so
the analysts devise flows that are suitable for computer processing,
but only after justifying, establishing, and simplifying the systems
themselves to maximize their utility. Obviously systems impinge on
a number of departments in the company. When the departments
change in a reorganization, the systems too may have to undergo
accommodative revision, at the least: different origins for computer
inputs, different distribution of outputs.

Along with systems changes may go revision of standard procedure
instructions—those big-company manuals that to assure uniformity
and security specify, for example, how a request for a market research
survey is to be initiated, processed, and executed.

Even training manuals may require revamping. For example, an
overhaul of the sales department may necessitate rewriting the procedural section of the sales training manual.

File management, too, must not be overlooked. With a decision to
turn the company's real estate activities over to an outside agency
comes another one on where the company's copies of deeds and leases
are to be assigned. Regrouping the company into separate lines of
business or product divisions requires sorting unified correspondence
files into, so to speak, separate heaps for each sales, marketing, engineering, and materials management section.

None of these small potatoes are apt to command much attention
from the Initiators of a reorganization, and in the press of other
matters, they may meet with various degrees of muddle, postponement, and discord among those afflicted with them in the lower offices
of the organization. Yet they must have some utility, for why else
would they still exist? Newly placed bosses may have some ideas on
revising them. The Planner may wish to set up post T-Day meetings
of those concerned to thrash out schedules for dealing with revisions.

POLICIES

Akin to the company procedure manual is the statement of written
policies—not those that governed the transition but those that express
the company's continuing character. In some companies these are
embodied in a manual which includes both company-wide policies—
"It is the company's policy to observe fair and legal hiring practices"—and departmental policies—"It is the purchasing department's policy that individual purchases over $3,000 must be supported
by written price quotations from the vendor," or "It is the research
department's policy to undertake only projects that have been requested in writing and approved by the research review committee."

Upon reorganization a company should reexamine its policies for both relevance and compliance.

Relevance of company-wide policies deserves attention at the top. Often these policies are promulgated by the president. In small companies they may emanate directly from the president's desk—not always in writing, sometimes in an occasional letter or bulletin. In larger companies they may be more formalized, originating, for the president's signature, from a policy committee or from division heads. At reorganization time these top-level policy enunciators should determine if the policies still hold true in the new company formulation. Some, such as not to discuss prices or marketing areas with competitors, undoubtedly will. But others may change as either a result or a purpose of reorganization. For example, "It is the company's policy to sell only through distributors," "It is the company's policy to make acquisitions only in lines of business that it is familiar with," "It is the company's policy to promote from within,"—the very purpose and act of reorganization may have been to reverse these policies.

Even departmental policies may undergo change as a result of reorganization. For example, an engineering department policy that "all drafting shall be performed internally" may become impossible to observe if an economy reorganization has halved the drafting department and its associated space. To change a policy that credit will be extended only to customers having a D&B rating of x or better may be the primary intention of a newly appointed credit manager. Out-of-date policies should be identified and reworded for the benefit of all who are subject to them.

Aside from policy change there is the matter of policy observance. Some policies are designed to protect the company against lawsuits and losses (legal compliance, for example); some to assure attainment of objectives (meeting any competitor's price, for example). As individuals enter new supervisory or managerial positions it is important for the company's welfare that they be aware of these policies. In the flurry of change they may never think of them. They may in fact act impetuously, with the best of intentions, in ignorance of them. But policy sets the direction and character of the firm. It is policy that distinguishes the super-cautious bank from the lend-to-anybody one; the quality-at-any-price manufacturer from the make-to-sell-at-a-low-price one; the ivied college from the diploma mill; the highly-paid skilled-employee manufacturer from the lower-pay high-turnover one. Those in charge should know and understand policy lest they introduce personal assumptions in its stead.

As soon as possible, then, the Planner introduces two sets of reviews. The first is a rereading of existing policies by every level of management. Those below the top level are asked to certify in writing that such review has been made. The second is a proposed revision of policies that are deemed inadequate to the company's new objectives. These should be submitted in writing for approval by the president or policy committee so that there will be general understanding and agreement on the reasons for a change in course. It is hard to see the point in a reorganization that results in no policy change, for it leaves the company essentially the same as before. In fact reorganization itself may be a violation of long-standing, unspoken policies on continuity. Perhaps such unspoken policies too should be articulated, in new form if necessary, in order to forestall mis-assumptions.

ODD JOBS

Following a reorganization a number of odd jobs must be taken care of. Most of these are handled directly by supervisors without prodding. They may, however, spur a temporary rush of work for responsible departments. Some examples are:

- Putting a hold on new hires (first and foremost in a retrenchment)
- Ordering new letterheads and business cards (and disposing of old ones)
- Applying for or transferring memberships in country clubs, dining clubs, and trade and professional associations (and cancelling old ones)
- Providing credit cards to newly entitled employees
- Reassigning parking and garage slots
- Changing address names on subscriptions to periodicals
- Transferring possession of company cars
- Changing locks or lock combination codes on sensitive property; changing computer access codes
- Authorizing admittance to company suites, public warehouses, safe deposits, and other off-site premises.

In addition to these fairly routine matters there is the release of the various notifications described in the Public Relations phase of the get-ready activities.

Furthermore, and far from petty, there is the immediate need to establish outside suppliers for the services of discontinued departments. If the in-house print shop is being closed down, for example, an external printer must be selected and put on call. If the company tool shop has been eliminated, an independent tool manufacturer must be located. For these activities some time may be required. Hence, the internal shutdown may have to be phased in with the external start-ups. Arranging for these transitions to be scheduled by those responsible is yet another of the Planner's occupations.

If the tasks described in this chapter have anything in common, it is their transience. They spring up in the wake of a reorganization as stones surface behind a plough, they are picked up, and that is the end of them. They have nothing to do with the objectives aimed for in a company overhaul. But there are other follow-up activities that do bear on the success of reorganization, and these we will consider in Chapter 15.

14

Reorganizing the Smaller Company

Unlike animals, small companies differ from large ones in more than size. In the animal world a mouse has about the same internal organs as an elephant. But in the business world the small company has a structure that in comparison with large companies can only be described as primitive. What big has to have small may well do without. A very small company may have little structure at all. Up front there is the owner and an office with three all-purpose clerks. Behind the dividing wall lies the shop, with its foreman and workers. And that is all there is. For now.

A somewhat larger company with several hundred employees tends to display more internal structure. This structure, however, is still far from that of its still larger cousins. Where the really large company has departments, this one has single-function employees. It has one person for example, to do all the purchasing, whereas a large company has fifty people for that purpose. The smallish company goes to an outside lawyer for patent work. The larger one has its own patent department. It is in this rudimentary structure of the small company that the seeds for future reorganizational problems lie.

FORMALIZING THE STRUCTURE CAN CAUSE PROBLEMS

For example, let us look at a manufacturer of computer adjuncts. Under the guidance of CEO Harry White, an electronics engineer, it has been forced by its growth to reorganize several times. New functions previously handled informally by almost anyone have segregated out into small departments, and White can not help noticing how things have changed. For example:

- There is Purchasing, which used to be handled on the side by Maybob Smith, the office clerk. Now it comes under a director of purchasing, Maybob herself, in fact. When the maintenance foreman rushes up to her desk, as he would in the old days and says, "Quick, Maybob, I need 200 feet of six-inch cotton belting!" she coldly replies, "Not without a written requisition—and from the parts inventory department, not from you. Don't you read the standard procedure instructions?" "Please, Maybob!" "No way. Against the rules." As a result the whole second shift in the assembly department has to be sent home. The foreman has transgressed departmental boundaries.

- Word has come back to the CEO that Joe Blue, the vice president of sales and one of the original gang, is ridiculing to customers the new vice president of marketing, a division that has recently been hacked out of sales. Blue resents the new department. But what does this look like to customers? And another thing: It used to be that customers with a problem could talk directly to Blue. Now, White has learned, they get shunted from department to department without ever getting a satisfactory answer. The personal touch has been lost.

- Not so long ago the personnel department was a set of card files on Maybob's desk. Now it is a department head and two employees, both of whom seem presently to be rewriting job descriptions and composing employees' manuals. Why?

- When the firm was young, people used to keep records by hand, and if a letter was needed and the CEO's secretary was busy, they pecked it out themselves on a typewriter. Now there are word processing operators in every department, and file cabinets and tapes to hold what they produce. There is even a mailroom, or "communications department," as it appears on the organization chart, run by a customer's drop-out son and not too accommodating, a matter that no one seems able to handle. White will have to deal with it when he gets back from a meeting with his financial underwriters. Pettiness has come aboard.

- There was a time when White, seized by an idea for a design change, would wander into the shop and get one of the operators on the line to try it out. Now he has to go through the manufacturing manager, who will not do anything without a drawing from the engineering department, which in turn must be checked by the research department and the quality department, none of which has more than three employees. Somehow an idea hardly seems worth hauling through all these departments. The fun has gone.

White sighs as he thinks of the happy family he once had, now grown up into a pack of departmental duchies, populated by strangers, sparring with one another, insisting on their rights, and performing strange rituals. And in the meantime the profit margin has dropped and newer, smaller, low-overhead competitors are nipping at his business.

And unless White is careful, things will get worse. The chief executive of a small company is in control—while it is small. He or she positions employees and says what they shall do. But as the company grows the CEO loses touch, and it changes. Departments assume prerogatives and duties. New departments and new managerial levels crystallize out of the solution, and what was once a smooth fluid turns into an impenetrable rock. Departments themselves cannot be blamed for this. Each is in fact trying to do its own thing as best it can. If anyone is at fault it is the top echelon, by failing to control the organization's growth. In a well-run company the chief executive designs the organization as neatly and sparely as its engineers and scientists design the product.

Somehow in a series of spontaneous and ad hoc reorganizations, White's small company has managed to get overorganized. It is a tadpole trying to act like an elephant.

REORGANIZATION SIGNALS

Smallish companies suffer many vicissitudes. Some of these spring from internal conflicts, some from the natural processes of growth, some from the difficulties of finance. Any of them may lead to reorganization. And this reorganization, though small scale, is effective only to the extent that it is thoughtfully carried out.

As an example of internal conflict, consider a company owned and operated by members of a family. Not infrequently those who started out by loving and helping, end up at one another's throats. They cannot agree on any aspect of the business. What one undertakes to do the others oppose. If their spheres of action overlap, employees receive contradicting instructions. As long as a dominant founder heads the company, conflict is at least held within bounds. But when this Jovian figure goes, a war of the gods breaks out, with all its discord and competition. To solve the problem two reorganizational actions are available: either reduce the number of family participants or get them to agree to strictly defined boundaries.

In the course of a small company's growth another not dissimilar form of internal conflict may arise. Through the demonstration of ability and the operations of the pecking sequence, some individuals move up from within into positions of semidominance. Though there is no formal organization chart, everyone knows that Bill is in charge of sales and Marge pretty much manages the small assembly and shipping department and Hans takes care of the people in the office.

Except that Bill and Marge and Hans fill in for one another when one is absent, and each freely moves in and out of each other's territory. By and by the company gets a little larger and more salaried employees appear. Bill has a few salespersons under him, Marge has two subordinate supervisors, and Hans has eight office employees. But they still practice mutual interference. The time has come to institute some order in this small chaos. This may not call for job descriptions and charts. A joint meeting recorded in a working agreement provides the desired blend of differentiation and cooperation. A delineation of accountabilities and responsibilities is made, the first step to organization.

Some smaller companies must also reorganize in response to danger signals. Often these reorganizations, though seemingly in a downhill direction, are essential for survival. For example, a 350-employee manufacturer of disposable hospital goods faces a loss of sales volume: a competitor has brought out a better syringe. One product means more to a small company than to a large one. Obviously, with fewer products to manufacture layoffs will occur in the shop. But the office too must be looked at. Are as many people now needed as before in such areas as Personnel, Accounts Receivable, Communications, Purchasing, and all the other functions that a higher sales volume justified? Perhaps what were once departments will collapse into one-desk jobs. Like a woodchuck going into hibernation, the company slows down its internal metabolism until Research comes up with a new product. And in so reorganizing it tries to preserve core functions at their minimum level so that key skills will be available to handle hoped-for reexpansion later on.

Retrenchment may also be needed to combat less-than-expected cash flow, the bane of small businesses. Too often a small business gets a good grip on its market, builds sales, optimistically staffs up to handle the volume, and then finds it cannot carry its debts. All those sales, and no earnings. If only it could add to its sales force, increase its advertising and promotion budget, and acquire facilities to turn out more goods, it might be able to surmount its fixed expenses. But where is the money for these daydreams? Money is what is short. Raise prices? The sales manager shakes his head sadly. Internal pruning and reorganization must be faced.

In the hospital goods case loss of sales justified shrinking of employment. But in the last case sales and production volume have hung steady. It will be more difficult to meet their demands with fewer employees. Yet if financial economy rules, this may have to be done. So as a result this retrenchment presents a far more sensitive problem than the previous one. There, fewer people made sense when there was less work to be done. Here, fewer people must shoulder the same workload. But employees do not easily accept a heavier individual burden because of financial problems that they had nothing to do with, especially when they see the owner's Mercedes sparkling in its reserved slot outside the window. Reorganization to a lower level must be neatly executed.

Reorganizations associated with growth are more healthy. The company may, for example, have reached that stage when it is crossing the well-known threshold. Owners are preparing to delegate responsibility to others. No longer does Harry White pause in his walk through the shop to show a spot welder how to position a part. He has relinquished that job to someone else, just as he has quit phoning suppliers since Maybob was placed in charge of Purchasing.

The need for threshold reorganization is not always easy to recognize and sometimes even harder to accept. But there comes a time when things left undone, or done wrong, or done at cross-purposes are difficult to ignore. The owner becomes frustrated, cannot handle all his or her time demands, sees nothing but subordinate incompetence, and perhaps has health problems. It may be that his bankers, his consultant (if any), or his customers will have to persuade him to delegate. Delegate how? By assigning authority, responsibilities, and accountability to specific positions—that is, by organizing. And as the company takes on girth not everything will be assigned to promoted insiders. Professional managers having specific skills will be brought in. To accommodate them, reorganization will occur. Then if, as often happens, the newcomers do not hit it off, they will be replaced, and reorganization may again have to be contemplated for new coalitions. Threshold reorganization is one of the most difficult for employees to endure, for it brings change and change again in the accustomed habits that had in fact made the company successful in its early stages.

Another fomenter of reorganization in smaller companies is the introduction of new activities and functions. For example, a decision to emphasize marketing may call for the entry of a new manager along with a scission of related activities from the sales manager. Or modest vertical integration—say, setting up a department for in-house cutting and forming of shipping cartons—may trigger a rearrangement of assignments in the manufacturing, quality control, and maintenance departments. Or the institution of a training director for hourly employees raises questions of reporting—should the director be part of Manufacturing, Administration, Quality, or Personnel? Small companies, as they evolve, not only pass through thresholds, they increasingly find specialists for what was never done inside before, or if done, done part-time. This continual fitting-in of new fields of concentration is a rolling process. Eventually the tiles laid one-by-one do not make the most attractive mosaic that could be desired. Reorganization becomes necessary to permit them to interrelate as they should.

Picking up new activities is another of the changes that business growth either makes possible or (as in the case of marketing) may necessitate. Along with it comes an expansion of existing activities. What were once single jobs swell into groups of people. Each group comes to have a "head person" leading it. The personnel file grows fatter. The office moves to larger quarters. Additional equipment and work tables appear in the shop, with additional people to labor over them. In response to customer requirements product lines are extended; additional sizes and grades get into the price list. With more people and more complexity an organization begins to form and subdivide. Departments arise. To whom should they report? How should they interact? How large should they be? In time what grew spontaneously must be assembled into a more effective and economical structure—it must in fact be reorganized.

Another stimulus for reorganizing: a small and profitable company undertakes a change in direction. It decides to abandon some of the less remunerative goods and services it has been selling and place more emphasis on the money lines. Or it adds a related but nevertheless different set of wares to its shelves. For example, a manufacturer of safety equipment decides to get out of fire-resistant clothing while broadening its line of protective headgear into the sports area. And to remodel its line it has to remodel its organization.

These examples show that smaller companies, being at once more vulnerable and more exploratory, are apt to attempt new internal configurations as readily as reason dictates. The need signals the change. And because they are small they are easily understood and easily manipulated, unlike corporate conglomerates whose complexities no one can realistically comprehend. Nevertheless, even small-company reorganization calls for navigational skills.

OBJECTIVES

A small company preparing to reorganize itself should, just like a large one, set down its objectives. The head of the company has undoubtedly been inclined to reorganization in order to cope with difficulties or exploit opportunities. What are these? How is reorganizing expected to take care of them?

The objectives may be any of those described earlier. Additionally they may include such specifics as:

• Fix more precise individual accountability for results

- Clarify who has authority over whom
- Introduce position ranking as an adjunct to salary rationalization
- More clearly distinguish exempt from nonexempt positions
- Divorce upper-level positions from trivial demands so as to free up time for important activities
- Integrate new or expanded activities
- Prepare for transition to outside-derived professional management
- Convert to an amplified level of operations in response to sudden sales growth
- Consolidate random islets of activities for cost reduction
- Initiate transition from generalized to specialized duties in order to build expertise.

Just as with a large company, the reorganization objectives should be written down at the start. Then when a plan takes shape it should be back-checked against them to be sure that it does in fact accomplish what was wanted.

POLICIES

In a large company the guidance of reorganization policies helps to preserve a certain unity of approach. It suppresses wrangling and uncertainties that would otherwise impede the development of a workable plan. When great numbers of people are involved, policy's forethought keeps everyone rowing in the same direction.

Written policy may be of less use in the smaller company. One thing that small companies have over larger ones is their flexibility. They can act ad hoc rather than according to rule. In formulating a reorganization the Planner—probably the president of the company—may have a few general precepts in mind: be fair to individuals, do not add more than can be afforded, preserve opportunity for participation, group kindred functions, focus accountability, do not do anything that will obstruct further change, and the like. But preexisting policies may not need to be in place. In fact, the very purpose of reorganization may be to express new policies. For example, setting up an off-site factory or a new store may reflect a new policy that reorganization embodies. Moreover, in a small company many reorganization policies essential for the large company—those on confidentiality, phasing, and personnel matters, for example—fall naturally into the president's thinking and will almost automatically be adhered to.

It is in the nature of many small companies to be undergoing frequent change; sometimes up, sometimes down. Whatever the direction, it may well determine policy far more effectively than policy will affect reorganization.

ORGANIZATION CHARTS

Small companies are not constrained to imitate large ones. For example, a largish company almost has to have an organization chart to find its way around inside itself. It inevitably develops departments and hierarchies. For smallish companies such organs may be superfluous.

The great advantage that small companies have over their bigger cousins is informality. They can respond and adapt quickly to sudden demands. And there is no mystery about them. Everyone knows what everyone else can and usually does do. You do not need a piece of paper with lines on it to stipulate, perhaps wrongly, where employees belong.

However helpful organization charts are to the large company, they can trip up the small one. In a large company those blocks on the chart, called "departments," are there to delimit areas of responsibility. In a small one they are counterproductive. They compartmentalize in a situation where open planning is more effective. They nurture internal rivalries and prerogatives: employees vying, as in Harry White's firm, more with each other than with competition. If one department head gets a new chair, they all want new chairs. In a small company reorganizing may mean adding, subtracting, or reassigning employees. It may mean inserting new functions or regrouping manufacturing layouts. If no departments have been formally recognized, all these changes slide into place without recarpentering a lot of artificial department walls.

This does not mean that the company is inhabited by an undisciplined mob. There are indeed specified areas of responsibility. The person who balances the books is not meddling in sales. Some districting is essential. But it should arise from mutual understanding and the nature of the work. If it does not, no chart full of boxes will impose it.

Nor does it mean that no one holds positions of authority. A major purpose of reorganization may be to enrich the company with even more authority: to bring in a CPA to handle accounting, for example, or a postdoctoral scientist to direct the research program. But to accomplish these purposes one need not Balkanize the company.

Neither should it be necessary to assign flattering titles too soon. To lard a company with general managers, associate managers, senior managers, supervisors, foremen, and directors of this or that may be a sort of psychological substitute for low salaries. It may even induce an identity-based sense of responsibility. At the same time it sets up headaches for the future. If you have called Watson, who handles the printing and mailing of brochures, "Director of Marketing," a bit of harmless window dressing, what title will you give the MBA professional that you hire some day to develop a real marketing program? And how will you go about correctly retitling Watson as "Mailing Coordinator?" Or suppose that in an attempt to look big-time you have liberally distributed "manager" titles to a host of functions. What have you done but installed needless vertical partitions between those functions, and horizontal ones between them and lesser jobs? Just because the military makes good use of titles does not mean that small or even medium-sized companies need them. Many companies in Italy get along *molto bene* without titles at all in the middle ranks. Where an American company would put: Manager, Receivables—P. De Leon, an Italian company would put only: Receivables—P. De Leon.

It is understood that De Leon is in charge of receivables. De Leon is *responsabile*, to use a word that is similar in both languages. And that is all that is needed.

By the same token, too much job description may do more harm than good. Large companies need job descriptions for a variety of reasons that never turn up in the smaller ones—job evaluation, instruction, employment, and performance appraisal, to name a few. The write-ups tend to be fairly detailed. The description for an envelope-stuffer operator, for example, may cover that job so narrowly as to apply to no other. But who wants that degree of particularity in a small firm? Descriptions, if used at all, should be couched in general terms that define only the rough skill levels required. "Perform various clerical and related functions as instructed," for example. Or "operate machine and shop tools to produce parts and make repairs from drawings, sketches, or oral instructions as to results."

As for standard procedures—the small company postpones them. Who needs them when everyone is within talking distance? As long as a small company stays loose, it can do without charts, titles, job descriptions, and all the other appurtenances of larger enterprises. It will then be in a position to conduct future reorganization without a sledgehammer.

It might seem then, that if the employees in a company interact in such purposefully ill-defined ways, there is scarcely an organization at all: hence nothing to be reorganized. In a way this is true. And yet even in such a situation, reorganization, regardless of what it is called, can sometimes unravel the tangles; for example, when that company run by squabbling relatives carves out areas of authority for each—

say, sales, manufacturing, and administration. Reorganization helps the company to contract, grow, or strike out in new directions. Even a reorganization of looseness may be initiated by an overworked president: in order to get people out of his hair he appoints a few key subordinates reporting directly to him, through whom all other contacts will be funneled. This is minor but effective reorganization. For a small company it is all the easier if overelaboration of structure has already been avoided.

SMALL TO BIGGER

At some point the successful small company matures to a point where skeletal structure and new differentiations of function and assignment must be dealt with. The tadpole is turning into a frog. Perhaps rising sales, the extension of territories, and the introduction of new product lines are moving the company out of its little pond. It may, for example, realize that it is no longer small when it has to buy a second copying machine.

Now reorganization may have to split the employees into well-defined groups, each with its own specialty. This first agglomeration is a tricky period. Intended to improve performance, it may instead create damaging internal barriers that slow things down. In it are laid the first seeds of future rivalries, distancings, and perquisites. Administration begins to nucleate out of the mass, bringing with it indirect expenses far removed from the direct costs of making and selling that were the small company's main outlays. Expanding overhead is in fact eating into the space between price and cost to make and sell. And as Harry White noticed, people seem to get more self- and position-oriented than company-oriented. All these are the shudders of breaking through the sound barrier. There is a time when the small company, growing, suffers a change in character. If reorganization recognizes this cross-point it may be able to soften the change through painstaking adjustment.

HUMAN ASPECTS

The human emotions that accompany working life are not ends in themselves. No one runs a company with the ultimate purpose of making people happy. Rather they try to keep employees happy so that the company will run well. (Presumably the better it runs the happier they will be.)

Nevertheless human considerations are never to be overlooked in reorganizing. Though the small company may not get into all the procedural niceties of a large one—organization charts, for example—

it should still observe many of the reorganizing procedures described for the large one.

Thus, the reorganization is carefully planned in advance. Its objectives are written down. Its changes are laid out on a chart that may later wind up in the president's desk drawer as a work sheet. The new duties of each *responsabile* are itemized. Salaries of individuals, properly interrelated, are specified. Talk memos are composed to be sure nothing is overlooked. They include, if appropriate, mention of reasons for change, plans for growth, and introduction of new abilities and people. Just as in a large company, the president tells his immediate subordinates and they tell theirs. A group meeting with all employees may renew consensus. A conscious effort is made to have the reorganization be understandable, acceptable, and encouraging. As in a large company, follow-up is not overlooked.

Small-company reorganizations are not small events. They prepare the way for advance into further ones. If they are well planned and carried out subsequent changes will not have to pick up what was missed. If they are performed with attention to the potentials of well-treated human beings, they will be stepping stones to a successful future.

15

Getting Restarted

Two kinds of unhappiness or one kind of happiness may permeate a company that has just been reorganized.

One kind of unhappiness: the employees suspect that the reorganization is only the first stroke in a lightning storm of further shake-ups. They do not feel safe in their jobs. They cannot figure out where the company is heading. Is their employer in deep trouble? Does anyone attach value to their work? What will happen to them in the next outburst of change? They have survived one cataclysm; what will become of them in another? Even if the reorganization is a phased one, with the general nature of next phases spelled out in advance, insecurity prevails. If unsure workers slack off in effort and quality; if foolish salespersons convey unease to customers, the company as well as its people suffers. In this atmosphere dire warnings from management of the need for greater productivity and profitability only exacerbate distress.

A second kind of unhappiness: Oblonskian confusion. Departments have been dismantled and the parts are lying about still unassembled. Transferred employees have not got a handle on their new jobs. Supervisors are not sure of their authority or in some cases of what they are expected to accomplish. If there has been a purge, the remaining employees are bewildered as to how they are to pick up the work of those who are gone; the librarian, for instance, stares at a mounting pile of technical reports and wonders how to get them all filed and indexed lacking the assistant who formerly shared the task. The merchandise manager sees customers roaming about looking for salespersons who are no longer on the floor. In the offices orders, invoices, and test results accumulate and no one knows what to do about them. The stationery stock department has been discontinued in favor of an outside supplier with daily deliveries, but no one knows how to go about ordering a replenishment of Form 1021. Not reorganization but disorganization comes from ill-communicated, ill-planned company convulsions, and if employees are unhappy with its demands on them, management is unhappy with its effects on performance.

One kind of happiness: employees quickly learn what is expected of them, superfluous functions have been thinned out, the most competent cadre of people remains, the company is once again focused on results rather than restructuring, and the prospect of prosperity fends off further alterations. This kind of happiness descends only upon a reorganized company that is consciously dedicated to its attainment. A mere reorganization solves no problems in itself. It is not the surgery but the postoperative recovery period that gets the company on its feet. Let us look at aspects of this convalescence.

MISSION AND GOALS

A first priority is telling people what is expected of them in the new company world. The reorganization has certain stated objectives. What must employees do to attain them, now that the way has been cleared? For example, suppose a retail chain was restructured to reduce the current number of outlets per area supervisor, so that each supervisor would have more time to develop additional stores. Then each supervisor must know this and set up timetabled goals for new openings. If a new lab has been opened to invent improved manufacturing methods for micro-chip substrates, the head of that lab must be told how the lab will relate to other departments and what should be accomplished, by what date; perhaps asked to prepare a plan of attack, with a rough protocol for each project. If commercial loan processing has been pulled back from branch banks into regional headquarters, the vice president of this activity should agree that the change must be sensitively handled with the branch managers, fully defined as to separation of function, and communicated to customers; with a reduction in expense and a growth in business. If two activities—say, Pricing Correspondence and Sales Planning—are being combined under one head, that supervisor must be told what outcomes are desired from this integration. The general objectives are translated into specific, definable results.

This communication of mission begins with the president and his or her vice presidents. It may consist of three parts:

First, the president may compose a "mission letter" to each vice president. The letter recalls those general objectives that bear on this vice president's area. It reviews past problems of that area that are now to be corrected. It addresses specific new difficulties and risks which, if they arise, must be counteracted. It outlines the positive improvements that the recipient will accomplish, with priorities. It stresses the need for taking concrete measures to enlist the productive cooperation of personnel subordinate to the vice president. It closes with an upbeat assurance of confidence and support.

The second part consists of a personal review between the letter writer and the recipient. In it there is a give-and-take discussion of both problems and expectations. The president clarifies and expands on individual elements of the letter. The vice president discusses alternatives and means of accomplishment. The meeting ends well when there is a clear sense of the mission and a mutual commitment to success, along with a personal rapport that will foster continued good relations.

The third part of the communicating process crystallizes the general mission into specific goals. After perhaps a week for the president and vice president to become more familiar with what the reorganization has wrought, the two meet again to agree on particularized future consequences. For each component of the overall mission they will articulate a real-world, real-time goal. For example:

- "By September 1 the distributor sales force will be augmented by forty new sales persons calling directly on stores with purchases in excess of $300,000."

- "By January 1 all offices and factories will receive operational audit in addition to the present financial audit."

- "By January 1 all policies over $1,000,000 will be reviewed by home office, instead of regional, underwriters."

- "Within one year joint-participant workplace assembly will replace conveyor line assembly, with no loss in quality or increase in cost."

- "In the next eight months an attitude survey in the stock transfer department will have disclosed reasons for employee hostility and corrective measures will have improved productivity by 10 percent."

- "By the end of the fiscal year the newly organized product divisions will be fully integrated, with no loss in market share."

Without such written goals the segments of the organization may easily, after T-Day, wander about on their own random paths. With them they discipline themselves to aim the specific results that will realize the reorganization's objectives.

Having occurred at the top, the three-stage mission process is carried down the line. The vice presidents repeat it with their subordinate managers, and they in turn with theirs until each department has agreed to its own particular marching orders. Conceivably the mission-transmission ends when the night maintenance foreman has worked out with the office cleanup group leader how to deploy the reduced force to keep the rearranged offices clean.

This total communication expansion is something like converting a simple melody into an orchestration for full ensemble, which when it is done results in an individual score for each desk in the orchestra, the third violins having their sheet of notes to play and the tympani their different ones. When the baton is raised for performance, musicians are prepared to play the right music for their particular instruments, in turn and in time with all the others. Improvisation is not wanted. The Planner, though not necessarily an orchestrator, must still at least be sure that the appropriate scores are distributed to all the players before performance begins.

RERELATING

Once the managerial and supervisory staff have accepted their commissions, so to speak, they cannot relax in a comfortable "now I'm safe and it's business as usual" euphoria. Department heads over groups of employees must attend to business-oriented human relations, for any of a variety of problems may have arisen. For example:

- Some bosses have employees unfamiliar to them. They must get to know them and establish a productive relationship.
- Some employees find themselves on jobs different from those formerly held. They must find out what to do.
- Some employees have been demoted or passed over for promotion. They must be helped to submerge their feelings in concentration on the work at hand.
- Some departments seem to be faced with the same work load as before, with fewer people to handle it. They must do one of two things: (1) find ways to reduce the amount of work to be done, or (2) devise improved methods of doing it.
- Some departments have been created to perform an activity new to their part of the company. They must originate methods of procedure.
- Some departments have been dissociated from their former corporate position and assigned to a new division. They must develop new relationships, or possibly even new emphases and procedures in their new environment.
- Some departments have been spliced together. They too must originate new procedures and internal assignments.
- Some employees—those brought in from an acquisition, for example—are new to the company altogether. They must become acquainted both with fellow employees and with company ways of doing things.

None of these situations can be allowed to drift along unnoticed. Time may exaggerate rather than heal their scars. So an early-on responsibility of those in charge is to pull their people together, to see that they really understand their mission, and to motivate them to cope with their new environment, optimistically, competently, and productively.

How this is done may vary from company to company, even from department to department in the same company. Thus the head of one department may work out at his or her desk:

- What the overall purpose of the department is
- What prompts specific activities in the department, and with what authorization
- What the outputs of the department are to be
- What quality standards the outputs are to meet
- When or under what conditions outputs fall due
- What the flow of work is within the department
- Who in the department is responsible for each subactivity
- What productivity standards govern departmental work—outputs per unit of time, for example, or outputs by deadline date
- How the department's activities and employees interact with those of other departments
- What training is necessary for employees.

Having worked all this out solo the head then issues it by sovereign fiat to the members of the department. To the extent that the instructions are good ones and are followed, all will be well.

Other department heads, more in tune with the times, may arrange for joint participation in the getting-under-way process. They assemble a meeting of department employees (remembering to include that most important one, the secretary) and let the group, apprised of its mission and responsibilities, decide on internal work flow, work methods, and allocation of duties.

Which approach is chosen depends on circumstances. Group consensus may not fit a department of 100 employees processing mail orders. It may work well in a ten-person laboratory processing inspection samples. In a tradition-dominated company no one may feel able to lead or participate in flip-chart chat sessions. In a company already accustomed to organization development sharing, a czaristic approach may be intolerable.

Regardless of method, positive, declaratory steps must be taken to meet the challenges of changed duties, repositioned people, and either reduced or expanding resources. With T-Day behind them, everyone charts new game plans.

TRAINING PROGRAMS

As an adjunct to reorganization, follow-up training programs may be called for. Some of these may be specialized; for example, in a decentralization move, teaching regional employees how to handle procedures formerly performed at headquarters. They may be technical; for example, giving instruction in new equipment that has been brought in as part of the reorganization. They may be interactive: in a product-oriented reorganization, engineers, brand managers, financial analysts, manufacturing and quality managers, and materials logisticians telling each other what they do.

Most reorganizations are intended in one way or another to get the company into a better competitive position. To this end it may be desirable to arrange outside class attendance so that chosen employees can introduce the latest developments in their fields.

Acquisitions too may call for special instructive classes. At these, selected groups are informed of the brands, market position, and manufacturing and distribution aspects of the new company cousin in order to facilitate current or future integration. For the accounting and data processing departments there may be even more specialized assemblies, getting into the small details of unified systems.

New activities also call for special education. For example, that addition of store salespersons to the distributor sales force previously mentioned demands a thoughtfully developed introduction to the skills of this type of call. Sales training may have to set up indoctrination classes.

Supervisory training too must not be overlooked. Supervisors newly raised from the ranks need instruction in their new role. Managers with expanded responsibility can all handle their jobs more comfortably if they are provided with courses in how to manage variety. For example, the head of Electrical Engineering promoted to be manager of all Engineering must be weaned from his speciality and taught the subtleties of delegation and balancing conflicting and interacting specialties under him. Even for the experienced, refresher courses may stimulate new ways of dealing with reorganization's challenges. There is scarcely a community where such education is not available.

A reorganization rests on the expectation that the company will perform better than before. One should never assume that this will automatically come to pass without attention to employees. Whatever they do must be done better, often with fewer means than previously. Training in their duties is a *sine qua non* if they are to realize the potential that has qualified them to be participating members of the revivified company.

PSYCHOLOGICAL REDIRECTION

Throughout this book there has been a tone of authoritarianism: people upstairs decide what is to be done, people downstairs do as told. Behavioral scientists frown on this type of management. It is Theory X, not Theory Y. It is undemocratic and worse, unproductive. Better that employees be told merely the results expected and devise their own best way of producing them. Let a humanistic value system prevail, in which human dynamics are freed for conflict confrontation, interpersonal competence, and self-actualization. Despite the jargon this is by no means impractical. In fact it is desirable.

Now of course there are times when it just will not work. If the work force is being cut drastically you cannot expect the employees to conduct an informal poll on which of their fellow employees stay and which go, though they may know better than anyone who the good and not-so-good bosses are, from their point of view.

"Research," says Lyman K. Randall, "shows that subordinates are reasonably accurate in discriminating between an effective and an ineffective boss. They base their judgments on their own private experiences with the world of bosses."[1] But do you want to leave staffing decisions up to them? If the reorganization is an emergency measure imposed by a lender or acquiring company or new turn-around CEO, there just is not time for arriving at group consensus. And if the company has a long history of authoritarianism the employees are not going to walk in one door of reorganization as servile peons and come out the other wearing the togas of Roman senators. In some reorganizations a certain amount of dictatorship is unavoidable.

On the other hand, there are occasions when the practices associated with Organization Development (OD) support every outcome that could be wished from reorganization. If you are starting up a green-field automobile plant, for instance, participatory management and work design can be introduced before the opening of the gates. If you have a loose and happy group of employees in your computer components factory, they may well join in organizing to handle growth of the business. In both cases the situation creates the opportunity.

In other cases the situation actually necessitates group interaction. For example, a small owner-operated company populated with free-style generalists is absorbed into a large, procedural corporation. The managers and employees of the small one are going to be shocked and embittered by the impersonal bureaucracy of the large one. Similarly, the managers and employees of the large one are going to be intolerant of the haphazard hipshooting style of the small one. The financial numbers that made acquisition look good on paper may collapse under the impact of culture clash. Here the very preservation of sales and cost parameters may demand quick therapeutic action with professional assistance from an industrial behavioral psychologist. The two sides should be encouraged to confront their differences and discover the avenues to mutual adaptation. What must be overcome is not mere culture shock. There are systemic obstacles to a meeting of hearts and minds. To be blunt, some small companies get away with a lot that big ones, under a hundred regulatory eyes, cannot. They can make special deals for special customers. They can skimp on spending for plant safety. They can sit heavily on unionizing. They can practice some degree of adaptive bookkeeping. They can provide hidden perks to their executives. They can introduce ad hoc changes in product design and packaging. They can make spot purchases for price and availability and tailor their product to suit what was bought. They are as different from big companies as a kudzu vine is from an oak tree. Not all small companies are like this, but many are, and bringing them into a large company is somewhat like incorporating the members of the Preservation Hall Jazz Band into a symphony orchestra. The band does its thing best when it improvises; the orchestra, when everyone standardizes. So getting the members of the two companies to reach a mutual adaptation to one another's peculiarities is essential for the success of an acquisitional reorganization. It requires an OD effort at all levels. Without it there may be a burgeoning outrage, from vice president down to the pension clerk, that can only postpone whatever rewards may have been expected from merging.

And maybe we are not just talking large marrying small. Big can mismatch with big. For example, describing the difficulties of adjustment following Sears' purchase of the giant financial house, Dean Witter Reynolds Organization, Inc., the *Wall Street Journal* reports that "Sears' slower-moving retailing culture hasn't adjusted to the entrepreneurial requirements of investment banking and consequently is cramping Dean Witter's style in that area. Indeed, Dean Witter executives acknowledge clashes between the high-flying, go-getter attitude of some departed executives and the steady, customer-oriented philosophy Sears espouses."[2] If you want to put things together, you have to smooth the rough edges so that they fit.

Even where acquisition is not part of the change, OD attitudes may energize a reorganized company. As mentioned, bureau-hardened employees will not be able to metamorphose into new personalities on T-Day. And yet opportunities exist. For one thing, many companies have had OD in place long before reorganizing. Their employees are psychologically prepared to deal with a changing organizational environment. For another, companies with no formal OD program may yet have within them supervisors who have a natural aptitude for creating the personal interplay and assumption of responsibility that OD encourages and pockets of employees who have fallen into attitudes of openness, risk-taking, trust, and collaboration on their own. Where this is true, the redesigning of tasks and workflow enables these self-starting areas to get running without protracted cranking up.

But there are companies where neither natural nor taught principles of OD have ever prevailed. In them the introduction of OD guidance should be seriously considered. Something about them has brought them to the throes of reorganization. Perhaps it was simply the life processes of bureaucracy, which had perfected every function to the point of total inertia. Perhaps it was a preoccupation with the company to the exclusion of a changing environment. Environmental or competitive changes do not alone wreck a company: internal failure to recognize and respond to them does. This is what leads to reorganization—it is psychological. Now if the company does attempt to rejuvenate itself by reorganization, of what use is this if the same old psychology still persists? What use is decentralizing if no one is capable of assuming more responsibility? What use is paring down if managers are intent on rebuilding their empires? What use is combining departments whose employees have traditionally been at each other's throats? The very factors that led to reorganization may still persist, vitiating any expected payoffs, unless there is instituted, along with the new organization chart, an approach to a new psychology. This will not be a quick-step march over the hill. It is a long trek. But unless it is undertaken through patient OD effort some reorganizations may be scarcely more than a repackaging of the same old goods.

The best Organization Development operates from top to bottom of the company. But sometimes, at the top, it is a misdirected effort. Here, for example, is a large company whose top executives are a well-knit group, thoroughly in charge and deeply knowledgeable in the technology of the business. Through their efforts, in fact, it has grown to its present dominating, though no longer profitable, position. Now it has been raided and bought by a conglomerate, and the purchaser has had it examined by a consulting analyst. "Why," says the analyst, "the place may not be earning what it should on its assets, but it's like a safe deposit vault full of jewels. What you fellows want to do is close down ten factories, get rid of all your customer salespersons and go to distributors, cut out any product line that contributes less than 10 percent of sales, switch to subcontracting for services and product components, and release 8,000 employees." No attempts at psychological turnaround are going to help the executive group cope with this land mine. Front-line employees are far more adaptable to behavioral change, because it is personally agreeable and they can make better use of it, than Olympians who have prospered on the nectar of authority. It would be easier to pull the ripcord on those executives' parachutes than to revise their psyches.

With this exception, an infusion of industrial psychology in revamped companies that have not already tried it may be the very thing that makes reorganization objectives come true. It encourages new group loyalties. It sets free brainpower locked in the cage of past inhibitions.

WORKING AGREEMENTS

Organizations without conflicts among the rights and duties of interrelated departments are rare. Often resolution of these has evolved through custom and tradition over the years. There is joint consent on just how far one department (or employee) should go before it is trespassing in the territory of another. For example, it may be an accepted given that the training department in Personnel is responsible for all employee training—except that training in salesmanship is handled by Sales Training in the sales department. There is agreement on how one department should help another. For example, it may be a long-established practice that the physical distribution department selects its own warehouses for lease—but that the manufacturing engineering department provides facilities consultation even though warehouses are out of its orbit. There is an acknowledgement that departments will not work at cross-purposes. Branch banks, for example, undertake not to suggest commitments to local borrowers who should be handled by the regional loan production officer.

With the redistribution of personnel and the reordering of departments that accompany reorganization some of these understandings may disintegrate, while the need for new ones arises. They are scarcely momentous enough to demand the formulation of a policy or a standard procedure instruction; or to be included in a mission statement or job description. Yet they have to be clarified, if only to nail down who does what in a shared relationship.

One approach is for those departments that mutually have hands-on activity to agree on their respective impacts. This may be done through a "working agreement." Its purpose is to assure that departments recognize how to handle matters in which they have overlapping or interfacing accountabilities. Such agreement is essential in order to:

- Be sure each party understands what activities it is responsible for engaging in
- Be sure each party understands where it takes initiative and where it seconds the initiative of others
- Avoid working at cross-purposes
- Avoid duplication of effort
- Be sure that nothing falls between shared accountabilities because each party thinks the other handles it
- Ensure mutual support and cooperation on shared accountabilities.

A sample of a working agreement is shown in Figure 15.1.

Working agreements may be spontaneously initiated by the participants. Alternatively, the need for specific ones may be suggested by a higher executive who has observed instances of inadequate coordination.

They may derive from a get-together of the participants themselves or under the guidance of a third party—the Planner, an OD agent, or a Personnel representative. Outside assistance may help resolve differences of opinion.

Upon agreement they are reduced to writing. Usually the written agreement, once composed, is put away and seldom referred to. The act of creating it has settled the problem that led to it.

FOLLOW-UP ACTION

As the dust settles in the weeks following T-Day, the Planner visits as many departments as possible to be sure things are going as intended. The purpose is two-fold: to be able to report back to the Initiator on progress and to assist in correcting lingering malfunctions.

The Initiator—a president or division head—needs reports for several reasons. First, anyone who has set in motion a major overturn is bound to be wondering whether the move has produced organizational dementia or sanity. He or she needs any reassurance that is legitimate. This is particularly true if the Initiator must in turn report results to a higher level. If the cry is "All is well," that is a good thing to know.

Secondly, though the daily activities of their job tell Initiators what is going on at the upper levels of their organization, perception of more internal forces is limited. It is as if they are flying over a forest, seeing the tops of the trees but having no idea of what is going on down under the leaves. The Planner can report to them on how well the creatures on the forest floor are getting along.

Thirdly, intelligence about reorganization's progress prepares the

Coordination of Insurance And Employee Benefits

Purpose

To coordinate the efforts and expertise of the Insurance Administration Department and the Benefits Department.

The Agreement

1. The parties recognize the need for close coordination of the efforts of their respective departments.

2. The Benefits Department will give as much advance notice as possible of proposals for new or amended employee benefit programs which are to be recommended for Company management approval. This will allow the Insurance Department time to determine whether adequate insurance coverage can be purchased at acceptable cost.

3. Before approved benefits schemes are announced to employees, the Insurance Department will receive the precise detail of the scheme in order to obtain firm confirmation of insurability and cost.

4. The Insurance Department will assist in the development of benefit schemes by providing costings requested by the Benefits Department for alternative programs. This is particularly important in preparation for union contract negotiations.

5. The Insurance Department will bring to the attention of the Benefits Department new developments in insurance programs which may improve the employee benefit program.

6a. Claims by employees under benefit programs will be administered solely by the Benefits Department. Employee claim and coverage questions received by the Insurance Department should be referred to the Benefits Department. Claims administration includes direct contact with insurance carriers.

6b. In the event coverage of a claim is denied and initial discussions between the Benefits Department and the carrier do not resolve the question, the Insurance Department shall have jurisdiction over further negotiation with the carrier. The Benefits Department will be consulted and informed throughout these negotiations.

7. Selection of insurance carriers is the exclusive jurisdiction of the Insurance Department. Requests by the Benefits Department for coverage by particular insurance carriers will be given consideration by the Insurance Department in selecting coverage.

Agreed by: George Smith - Manager, Insurance Department
            Leah Jones   - Manager, Benefits.

Figure 15.1

Initiators for possible next phases. For example, if the reorganization is geared to growth, having it well in place means the company can safely commit itself to higher levels of sales and production. If it involves absorption of an acquisition, successful beginnings clear the way for a second assimilation. If it mandates retrenchment, assurance that the expected savings are well in place underwrites redirection of funds to other purposes—stepped-up advertising and promotion, for example. If it is a regrouping for faster internal response and sharper competitive thrust—product differentiation, for example—knowing that the troops are all in their respective bivouacs allows new strategic business plans to be put into action. The Initiator's goal was not reorganization itself, but what comes next. He or she needs to know when "next" can begin.

Aside from its advisory aspects, follow-up often discloses the need for corrective measures, for, as every air traveller knows, nothing ever goes quite as planned. Scouring through the company in the aftermath period, the Planner takes steps to rewire the board where flashing lights appear. For example:

- A few misfits have turned up. The research chemist promoted to an administrative position is suffering desk-shock. He wants to be back with his instruments and glassware.

- Essential arrangements have not been carried through. The Washington sales office, for example, was closed down all right, and the premises vacated, but no one thought about the local post office box, which is now in a state of advanced glut.

- Physical relocation is slowing things down. The hospital purchasing staff are sitting at desks in the hallway because their proposed office is torn up for new conduits.

- Some things have been overlooked altogether. That archives department mentioned in an earlier chapter, for example.

- Untoward events have occurred. The computer librarian, fired for ineptitude, has signalized her departure by erasing the customer mailing list tape.

- Personality clashes have arisen. The newly-appointed head of credit card debits has assumed a martinet persona, antagonizing the employees with a fire-and-brimstone introductory speech.

- Restructurings appear necessary. Both the materials planning department and the maintenance department agree that the maintenance parts inventory clerks should have been assigned to the latter, not the former, department.

- Inexperience shows up. The book production department, placed under an upward-bound MBA as a career-broadening assignment, is having a little trouble teaching their new boss the ropes.

Some of these problems will solve themselves quickly, some will dissolve in time, and some require immediate outside attention. The Planner finds out about them by talking to people. "How are things going here?" he or she asks. And then, more pertinently, "How about over there?"

Lucky companies do not have a lot of experience in reorganizations. So when one occurs it is bound to end up with a few unforeseen squeaks and rattles. By the same token, employees may be unduly alarmed by the smallest gremlin. To them it means that the whole undertaking has been a horrible mistake. One puff of steam and they think the reactor is in meltdown.

It is therefore important to detect and remedy any serious deviations from course as soon as they occur. It is for this reason that the Planner does not take off on vacation just after T-Day. Some one has to keep an eye on the gauges and perhaps report informally to the Initiator on new actions taken.

Morale, too, deserves follow-up in the ingoing days of the newly-reorganized company. The president may wish to assemble a mass meeting (either in person or on video) of employees to retell what has happened and why, to picture the company's strengthened position as their employer, to thank them for their cooperation and accommodation in the changes, and to encourage their continued efforts. The president might even undertake to answer questions from the floor. But a meeting may be impractical—then a letter from the president to all employees may still carry the same message. These measures help to dispel lingering anxieties and establish the company in its new architecture.

NOTES

1. Lyman K. Randall, "Common Questions and Tentative Answers Regarding Organization Development" in *A Practical Approach to Organization Development Through MBO—Selected Readings*, ed. C. A. Beck, Jr. and E. D. Hillmar (Reading, Mass.: Addison Wesley Publishing Co., 1972), p. 15.

2. *Wall Street Journal*, 13 Sept. 1983.

16

Organization Control

Of all reorganizations retrenchments are the most traumatic. They are disastrous for employees who lose their jobs. They are miserable for the bosses who have to do the firing. They at least temporarily overload the employees who are left. They often throw a burden on the community. Having experienced one, you certainly do not want to have to go through a second.

And yet some companies do. They have a big cutback now and in not too long they have another.

Reorganizations can be like a crash diet. The dieter trims off thirty pounds, self-congratulates, and resumes stuffing. Similarly, the company, having tossed out a lot of employees, goes back to business as usual. When it next weighs itself, surprise! It is overweight again. More toss-outs. A retrenchment reorganization that is only a crash program is not enough. Without continual discipline pounds will creep back on. Hiring resumes. Departments are created. New managerial positions steal in. After all the agony of closing plants and offices a subsequent acquisition introduces a new string of small factories and overheads. If a new president joins the company, the first thing he will think of is, "We must reorganize!" "Oh," think the employees, "not again!"

So a retrenchment, once completed, is in a precarious position. It is like a weeded garden. Everything looks nice and clean today. But if you turn your back on it the weeds start to pop up again. Soon the company is once again a tangled mass of undergrowth. Those very forces that once necessitated reorganization still prevail. And as they do they interfere with all reorganization's original objectives: profit growth, product emphasis, faster response, competitive thrust, and all the rest. They must be contained. Reorganization must be succeeded by rigid controls to preserve the gains achieved. For this purpose specific mechanisms are available. Let us look at some of them.

PAYROLL WATCH

One easy approach is to keep an eye on employment. How many people are getting current paychecks? Monthly figures are charted on a graph. When the graph starts climbing, trouble is ahead. Except....

Some businesses cannot expect to hold to a sea level of employment. They are seasonal—department stores, for example, or health institutions. They expect their employment graph to bob up and, desirably, down from time to time. They need a measure sensitive to legitimate causal factors. In such companies a ratio may be more desirable: number of employees per 1,000 dollars worth of sales, production, or shipment, whichever should govern employment. This is the ratio that management should try to hold horizontal on its graph.

But, it may be said, this is impossible. There is bound to be a cadre of permanent, fixed employees. When sales, production, or shipments dip, of course the employee ratio will rise. Good point. But this problem is convertible into a challenge. Perhaps one of the objectives of reorganization should have been to suppress fixed expenses—by minimizing the number of internal departments, for example.

Employment ratios should be compared with other indicators. For example, if the employment/sales ratio is outrunning the profit/sales ratio, something alarming may be going on. Maybe employment is eating into profits. There may be a good reason—staffing up for a sales drive or for product introductions. On the other hand, there may be a bad reason—relapse into old patterns of over-staffing for the amount of business at hand.

Another ratio that bears attention is that of employees to managers and supervisors. In a retrenchment program there is a two-fold effort: to reduce the number of employees and to broaden the span of attention of managers. For example, a supervisor with only a few employees is a waste of managerial salary. It does not take eight hours a day to manage three or four people. The supervisor must be, if not a total window watcher, performing nonmanagerial duties as well. But if this is the case, why pay for managing? An organization is lean when it has the least number of people necessary to guide others in the doing of things. It is bloated when it is filled with titular supervisors ruling tiny kingdoms. (One exception: when an employee manages a function rather than people, being accorded the title "manager"

POSITION CONTROL LIST		
Dept. Name: Sales Planning Dept. No.: 702 Date: 5/6/xx		
Job No.	Job Title	Authorized Incumbents
802	Manager	1
803	Planner	4
804	Market Administrator	2
805	Data Analyst	1
806	Promotion Clerk	1
807	Secretary	1

Figure 16.1

for prestige reasons—manager of press relations, for example.) Generally speaking, a small number of employees per supervisor suggests empire building. It also breeds a profusion of approvals, relay stations, order transmission, and petty bureaucracy. Worse, the more supervision the less opportunity for participative management by "doers," who are oppressed by "tellers."

POSITION CONTROL

The ratios we have mentioned are useful, but they have a deficiency. Theye are *ex post facto*. They tell what has happened. If what has happened is unfavorable, then you have to go in and do something about it. This takes time and it also creates a certain amount of dissension. It is better to have a way to hold levels at a predetermined norm before they can start creeping up. Position control provides such a mechanism.

With an "automatic" position control system each position is listed along with its authorized number of incumbents (see Figure 16.1).

Introduction of new positions or employment of incumbents beyond the authorized number is permissible only upon written authorization from the president. Such authorization is received only after (1) a written description of alternatives to hiring, and (2) a cost and savings estimate justifying the increase against alternatives.

A more drastic practice is to ban the refilling of vacancies without presidential approval. On the heels of a retrenchment this is severe treatment indeed. Yet it does force an effort at methods improvement as a substitute for routine hiring.

In both these cases dragging the president into the picture tends to suppress the number of requests made.

It should be noted that when a company is poised for growth—in the development or marketing of new products, for instance—the number of authorized incumbents may exceed the number actually on hand until the vacancies have been filled. At that time further hires are precluded by the authorized numbers.

In another special case fixed authorized numbers may well apply to the upper and middle ranks of the chart but not to bottom line positions. For example, the number of order-entry clerks in a mail-order house may vary with the volume of business. The allowed numbers are then geared to volume in a manner similar to that of a flexible budget.

PEOPLE APPROPRIATIONS

It is a curious fact that many companies, in this age of automation and robots, resist spending money on machines far more than on people. Typically a new piece of equipment requires an appropriation request. The capital expenditure must be thoroughly justified. Its necessity must be explained. Discounted cash flow is called on to determine the rate of return on the investment. Approval is granted only when the proposal has passed a series of hurdles, including upper-level review. Yet adding a new job is child's play. Thus, the chief engineer thinks it would be a good idea to have a backup energy analyst. His budget is no problem, for he has some padding in the travel account. He tells the employment department to start looking, and soon another name is added to the payroll. Often people are easier to acquire than machines.

There is something inconsistent about this. A middle-level professional may cost, with all overheads and fringes, an average of $75,000 a year. This expenditure over a five-year period has a present value (at a 10 percent discount rate) of about $285,000. Few companies would commit themselves to a machine at this cost without the most serious consideration. At the same time many would allow the equally expensive employee to be slid in after perhaps no more than a brief chat between the chief engineer and his boss.

Moreover, the machine, though harder to acquire, is no problem to get rid of. If the company wants to dispose of it, sale or writeoff will bring in a fillip of cash flow. By contrast, if it wants to relieve itself of the employee it may find itself incurring additional severance outflows. Employees can cost more than machines, coming and going.

Perhaps the acquisition of employees should be treated with as much circumspection as that of fixed assets. The company controller, rather than the personnel manager, may be the person to keep the employee roster in bounds.

For this purpose consideration may be given to a "People Request" not dissimilar to a capital appropriation request. Such a format would include:

- Statement of proposal
- Summary of benefits
- Description of alternatives
- Present value of additional five-year outlays, suitably escalated for inflation and merit increases
- Present value of five-year savings or added income.

The "people request" would require the same approvals as an appropriation request. Its mere necessity is an encouragement to improve systems and methods rather than add to payroll. And its string of approvals and reviews, distasteful to potential empire builders, discourages its casual use. In this particular instance a little dash of bureaucracy in the right place quells bureaucracy's growth in others.

DEPARTMENTAL APPRAISAL

Most of the "controls" discussed have dealt with people and positions which are, need it be said, but components of departments. And as we have seen earlier, departments are often the source of organizational problems. Preventive medicine may be needed for them too.

First, since proliferation breeds cost and excessive interaction, containment may be advisable. If a "people request" helps to restrict the payroll, a similar procedure may be used to suppress the growth of new departments. Thus a simple rule: no new department may be established, nor any existing one subdivided, except upon specific approval of the president of the company.

Another control measure helps to assure that those departments

DEPARTMENTAL APPRAISAL

Date	Department Name			Prepared By

Element	RATING			Recommendations or Action Plan * Reference
	100% Okay	Okay, But Could Improve	Not Okay-- Improvement Needed	
1. Properly placed in organization				
2. Accountabilities clear -- to members -- to other departments				
3. Duties clear -- to members -- to other departments				
4. Authority scope and limits clear -- to members -- to other departments				
5. Authority sufficient				
6. Internal structure clear and "minimum"				
7. Internal policies, procedures and rules clear				
8. Employees technically competent				
9. Backups available and being trained				
10. No excess of approvals, supervisory permission and review, etc.				
11. Work well-scheduled				
12. Work handled expeditiously; through-put time okay				
13. Quantity of output meets expectations				
14. Quality of output meets expectations				
15. Response to emergencies satisfactory				
16. Methods up-to-date				
17. Develops, acts on new ideas				
18. Cooperative and service-oriented -- to others in organization -- to external publics				

Figure 16.2

200

	Element	RATING			Recommendations or Action Plan * Reference
		100% Okay	Okay, But Could Improve	Not Okay-- Improvement Needed	
19.	Communications with others in organization adequate				
20.	Working agreements where needed				
21.	Positive response to suggestions				
22.	Physical assets well-maintained				
23.	Assets safeguarded				
24.	Safety record satisfactory				
25.	Budget satisfactory				
26.	Budget met				
27.	Costs/unit-of-output okay				
28.	Files/records adequate and organized				
29.	Physical location okay				
30.	Equipment adequate				

* This final column refers to written action plans which should include:

. Recommended change

. Statement of problem and its consequences

. Benefits of change

. Cost (if any) of change

. Ancillary problems (if any) associated with change

. Timetable for change

. Person(s) accountable for effecting change

. Positions/departments affected by or involved in change.

Figure 16.2 continued

that exist are performing effectively. A periodic performance appraisal and development plan similar to that for the individual employee may also be applied to a department. And it has its own merits—it is impersonal. Unlike that for the department head, it does not come down on one person's shoulders: it is spread among all members. Free of personal stigma, it is less threatening, more objective. Also, it evaluates far more aspects of the group—its behavior, its facilities, and its place in the organization—than does a personal appraisal of the supervisor's performance alone. The appraisal may be self-performed by departmental members or by the heads of other interacting departments. Sensitively introduced and executed, it leads to action plans for improvement. An example is shown in Figure 16.2.

THE VALUE OF CONTROL

From one point of view reorganizing a company is an exciting opportunity. It exercises the imagination. It sparks creative thinking: how might something be done better? It challenges accepted beliefs: do we *really* need such and such an activity? It unblocks dead-end career paths. It opens up opportunities for individuals to realize unused talents. It prepares the ground for new freedoms of initiative and participation. It releases new efficiencies in the use of resources. It smoothes the adaptive integration of acquired organizations into existing ones. It converts the company from internal to external orientation. It lofts the company into a growth and profit trajectory. But why should all this, delightful though it may be, have to be brought into existence? Why isn't it going on already?

Reorganization engenders stress. The company itself undergoes an upheaval that at least temporarily slows it down. Some employees struggle in more demanding situations. Some feel shunted aside. Some must forfeit their livelihood. Communities may lose a traditional source of employment and tax revenue. However exciting reorganization may be in some ways, it can be tragic in others.

What makes reorganization necessary? Torpid management. Management that lets the corporate population grow without limit. Management that allows its middle ranks to become an impenetrable tangle. Management that permits facilities to become passé; that holds on to old ones out of commitment to an irrelevant past; that tolerates multiple overheads for the sake of "flexibility." Management that reacts, too late, to changed customer needs rather than itself proactively creating them. Management that closes its eyes to new market and competitive challenges. It is with such management that a company finds itself, on the brink of disaster, faced with a disruptive reorganization.

Are reorganizations inescapable? Not at all. In a well-run company there is continual rolling adjustment to the business environment. Small internal restructurings are made to adopt improved technologies, to introduce new product lines, to extend sales reach. Obsolescent facilities and departments are quietly phased out rather than allowed to go downhill until crisis bombing is necessary. Always fine-tuning to its environment, the company sustains a gradual, evolutionary growth.

Such a company controls itself. It emplaces systems for detecting those changes in sales, share, and profitability that could herald, unless promptly dealt with, organizational revision. It resists departmental proliferation. It discourages employment inflation. It supports this anticipatory discipline with indicators and controls.

In a sense, a big reorganization is a disgrace. It is a public confession that management has let the company drift into deep trouble. But when it must happen, it should at least happen well—without hysteria—and permanently—without repetition. This book has attempted to describe an approach to reorganization that is both rational and as far as possible, humane. And it closes with the observation that a reorganization is in the end effective only if it is followed by controls that will forestall another.

Index

About the Author

STANLEY B. HENRICI is a retired Manager of Organization Systems for a major food processing company. His earlier works include *Standard Costs for Manufacturing* and *Salary Management for the Nonspecialist*, as well as articles in the *Harvard Business Review*, the *New York Times*, the *Financial Analysts Journal*, and numerous technical publications.